No-Thaw
Paleo Cooking
IN YOUR INSTANT POT®

No-Thaw Paleo Cooking

IN YOUR INSTANT POT®

Fast, Flavorful Meals
Straight from the Freezer

Dr. Karen S. Lee

Author of *Keto Cooking with Your Instant Pot®* and *Paleo Cooking with Your Air Fryer*

PAGE STREET
PUBLISHING CO.

PAGE STREET
PUBLISHING CO.

trustees

For Lori and Maura who are the epitome of the chief cook and bottle washer at work and at home. Your quest for quick and healthy meals led me to write this book, and you know I will always answer your texts and phone calls whenever you need my help, including why you keep getting the "Burn" message on the damn Instant Pot panel.

I am eternally grateful we are growing old together, with steaming Instant Pots in the kitchen, wine glasses in our hands and the fur babies at our feet.

I love you, always.

Contents

Slurping Noodles – 125

Steaming Soups and Stews – 143

Leaves and Roots – 173

Introduction

When my children were younger, I tried my best to be the super organized mom who never forgot anything. I had a full-time chiropractic practice, and I had two small children in two different schools whom I had to drive every morning—so it was a bit chaotic before I went to work. As you can imagine, sometimes dinner plans were foiled because I forgot to take the meat out of the freezer before rushing out the door. Regrettably, I'd resort to either macaroni and cheese from a box or takeout pizza. Things are different now because I can cook even frozen meat in the Instant Pot®, but I didn't have the luxury back then.

If you understand what I'm talking about, *No-Thaw Paleo Cooking in Your Instant Pot®* is for you. This cookbook is all about using the Instant Pot to help you put healthy meals on the table despite your busy life.

My family appreciates a good meal. Because of their food-related health challenges, we've been on the Paleo diet and they spend a great deal of time shopping, cooking and generally paying attention to what they eat a bit more than an average person. A few years ago, they asked me how they will remember my recipes. That's when I decided to start a specialty food blog so they could refer to all of our favorite recipes whenever they need them. Cooking Paleo meals can be challenging, but using tools and appliances such as the air fryer and the Instant Pot makes it easier and more fun. That led me to write *Paleo Cooking with Your Air Fryer* and *Keto Cooking with Your Instant Pot®*.

I included rice and potatoes in some of the recipes in this book because I wanted to write what my family normally eats. Technically, they are allowed on the Paleo diet; unless you have issues with any kinds of grains or nightshade, you can eat them occasionally like we do. If you prefer, you can substitute cauliflower rice or yuca or sweet potatoes.

For this cookbook, I have recreated many classic dishes, such as Healthy Beef and Vegetable Soup (page 147), Dump and Forget Chicken Cacciatore (page 17) and Honey BBQ Baby Back Ribs with Sweet Potato Fries (page 84) using frozen meat in the Instant Pot. And I've developed new recipes with frozen meats, such as Boneless Rib Eye Steak with Rosemary and Garlic Butter (page 65), Easy Peasy Coq au Vin (page 21) and Ropa Vieja with Cauli Rice (page 58). I am sure you are familiar with some of the classic recipes, but this cookbook will show you how to cook them straight from the freezer.

Cooking frozen meats in the Instant Pot is similar to cooking with fresh meats, but it requires more time and a couple extra steps. The most important thing to remember is to use a good meat thermometer to make sure the meat is fully cooked and has the right texture. There are more tips in the next section to help you successfully cook meats in the Instant Pot without thawing. These are important points that you should know to ensure great results, so be sure to read it fully before making any recipes in this book.

Now that my children are grown and can drive themselves, my mornings are not as hectic as they once were. But still, blogging, writing cookbooks, binge watching *Grey's Anatomy* and managing life in general can make meal planning just as complicated sometimes. So, I love that I can prepare meals on the fly using frozen meats—and I hope you'll love it too!

In your health,

Dr. Karen

No-Thaw Cooking Tips

My goal in writing this book is to share recipes you can cook using frozen meat in the Instant Pot. I want you to be able to serve tender, flavorful meals that are thoroughly and evenly cooked. To help you get started, I've come up with a few tips so you can cook successfully using the "no-thaw" cooking method in the Instant Pot on one of those busy days.

Meat Size—Theoretically, you could pressure cook any frozen meat by adding 50% more time, but it may not result in the best flavor or texture. A big chunk of frozen meat, such as a 3-pound (1.4-kg) chuck roast, might not cook thoroughly and evenly. Also, the texture will be less desirable than fresh meat. From my experience, cooking frozen meat that is 2 pounds (907 g) or smaller results in more even cooking and a more tender texture. If possible, buy a smaller cut of meat to freeze, or cut the meat into smaller portions before freezing. Remember, the meat size matters more than the total amount of food when it comes to pressure cooking.

Bone-In or Boneless—I use bone-in meat whenever possible because bones add more flavor. But for cooking frozen meat in the Instant Pot, I prefer boneless cuts because they cook faster. If all you have is bone-in meat in the freezer, use what you have and add 2 to 4 extra minutes to the cooking time, depending on the type of meat.

Inner Pot Size—Before you freeze any meats, make sure the full width of all the pieces is less than 8⅝ inches (21.9 cm) wide. This is the diameter of the inner pot of the Instant Pot. You also want to pay attention to the height of the pot (6⅓ inches [16 cm]) and be sure not to fill the pot more than two-thirds full. I usually take the meat out of the original package and freeze it in the shape and size of the inner pot, just in case I need to cook it without defrosting it.

Browning Frozen Meat—Yes, you can brown frozen meat! While the Maillard reaction—browning reaction of chemicals in food—for frozen meat may not be the same as for fresh meat, it still occurs—so try to brown as well as you can for richer flavor. Just be very careful when you add any frozen meats to hot oil, as it will splatter.

Food Safety—Take food safety seriously regardless of how you cook. Food safety is paramount, especially when cooking in the pressure cooker because you can't open the lid to check for doneness during cooking. For safety, always use an accurate thermometer to check for proper temperature. Chicken should be at least 165°F (74°C). Pork should be 145°F (63°C). Medium-rare beef should be 125 to 129°F (52 to 54°C) right out of the pot; as the meat rests, it should go up to finish at 135°F (58°C). There are many food thermometers on the market; in my opinion the ThermoWorks thermometers are the industry's best for their accuracy and precision.

Regardless of what the cooking instruction says about timing or the exterior appearance of the food, always remember to cook to internal temperature—not time.

Before Freezing—Take the meat out of the original packaging and wrap it well with freezer paper or place it in a container or ziplock freezer bag. Don't forget to remove the paper that lines the tray that the meat was packaged in. For a whole chicken, take out the gizzards from the inside cavity. Season the meat with spices and herbs, but do not salt the meat before freezing. Adding salt to the meat will draw out the moisture, making it dry and chewy when cooked; add salt right before cooking and not before freezing for a more tender texture. Be sure to label the container or the bag clearly. Frozen meats are harder to recognize, so clearly label the type of meat, weight and the date.

Frozen Vegetables—I like to buy vegetables when they are in season and freeze them to cook with throughout the year. But cooking frozen vegetables can be a bit tricky because not all frozen vegetables cook well. Frozen root vegetables do, and I usually buy beets, parsnips and even Brussels sprouts and freeze them. They cook perfectly every time!

Finally, although you can cook frozen meats in the Instant Pot, that doesn't mean they all taste as good as using fresh meats. The secret to making them taste as good is to flavor them with fresh herbs and spices. Of course, dried herbs are okay, but I try to use fresh herbs as often as I can for enhanced flavor, especially when cooking with frozen ingredients.

Carnivore's Cave

Meat dishes in the Instant Pot come out incredibly tender and flavorful. And some nights you have all the right ingredients ready to make an impressive meal for your hungry family. But if you're like me, there are more nights when you go, "Shoot! I forgot to defrost the meat!" . . . and then you panic.

So, if you are wondering what to do with a big chunk of frozen meat sitting in the freezer and no grand plans, don't worry. I wrote this long chapter on how to prepare delicious meals without thawing frozen meats just for you. Who am I kidding? I wrote this for me.

Cooking frozen meat in the Instant Pot is just like cooking regular meats, except you need a little creativity and maybe slightly more time to cook. And believe me, there are more important things in life than worrying about defrosting meat—so let me take the dinner worries off your plate.

The first step is to be sure to read my tips in the beginning of the book on food safety (page 11) to ensure the meat is cooked thoroughly, especially poultry and pork. So, are we good? Good.

You will love classics such as Braised Beef Shank with Citrus Gremolata (page 37), Boneless Rib Eye Steak with Rosemary and Garlic Butter (page 65) and Easy Peasy Coq au Vin (page 21). And dishes such as Barbacoa for Days (page 54), Chipotle Chili con Carne (page 57) and Carefree Carnitas Salad (page 83) are great as leftovers.

Make some of my classic meatball recipes ahead of time to freeze, and dump them in the Instant Pot for a really quick meal. You'll love the simple Chicken and Apple Patties with Cabbage Hash (page 27), Nona's Meatball Marinara over Zoodles (page 14) and Swedish Meatballs over Cauliflower and Parsnip Purée (page 61).

With these quick meal options that take just a slight bit of planning ahead, you don't have to panic later. See, you *can* get a delicious dinner on the table—even when you forget to defrost the meat.

Nona's Meatball Marinara over Zoodles

I bet no one makes meatballs better than your nona. Well, I beg to differ. After you try this Paleo version, you'll be shocked by how much better these are compared to your nona's. I credit my secret for making these moist—tapioca flour. Make batches of these meatballs and cook them fast on those nights when you don't know what to cook for dinner.

COOKING TIME: 12 MINUTES — SERVES 4

MEATBALLS

1 lb (454 g) frozen ground beef

½ cup (80 g) finely diced onion

1 tbsp (9 g) finely minced or pressed garlic

2 tbsp (8 g) chopped fresh parsley

2 tbsp (5 g) chopped fresh basil

1 tsp dried oregano

1 large egg, slightly beaten

1 tbsp (8 g) tapioca flour

1 tsp sea salt

2 tbsp (30 ml) extra virgin olive oil (EVOO)

SAUCE

½ cup (80 g) diced onion

1 tbsp (9 g) minced garlic

4 cups (720 g) crushed tomatoes

1 tsp Italian seasoning

Sea salt and freshly ground black pepper, to taste

3 zucchinis, spiralized

½ cup (40 g) grated Pecorino Romano cheese (optional)

2 tbsp (5 g) finely julienned fresh basil

To make the meatballs to freeze: In a medium mixing bowl, combine the ground beef, onion, garlic, parsley, basil, oregano, egg, tapioca flour (my secret) and sea salt. Mix well and form 1½- to 2-inch (3.5- to 5-cm) meatballs. You should be able to make about 12 meatballs. Place the meatballs on a tray, cover tightly with aluminum foil or plastic wrap and freeze. Store in a ziplock bag in the freezer up to 1 month.

When you are ready to make the meatballs in the Instant Pot, take the meatballs out of the freezer, and place them on a platter in a single layer.

Turn on the Instant Pot by pressing "Sauté" and set to "More." Insert the inner pot and wait until the panel says "Hot." Add the olive oil to the inner pot and coat the bottom evenly. Carefully add the meatballs and brown all sides. Cover the lid while browning as the oil will splatter. Cook them in batches, if needed. This should take about 5 minutes. Place the cooked meatballs on a plate and set aside.

To make the sauce, add the onion and garlic to the inner pot, and sauté for 1 minute. Add the crushed tomatoes and Italian seasoning. Add the meatballs back to the inner pot and cover them with the sauce. Close the lid tightly and move the steam release handle to "Sealing." Press "Cancel," then the "Pressure Cooker/Manual" button and set the timer for 5 minutes on HIGH pressure.

When the timer ends, allow the Instant Pot to cool down naturally for 10 minutes. Then, carefully turn the steam release handle to the "Venting" position for the steam to escape and the float valve to drop down.

Press "Cancel." Open the lid carefully and stir the sauce to mix with the meatballs. Add sea salt and black pepper, if needed. Add the zoodles on top, and do not mix. Close the lid and wait for 2 minutes.

Plate the zoodles in a shallow pasta bowl, place the meatballs on top and ladle the sauce over the meatballs. Sprinkle with Pecorino Romano cheese (if using) and garnish with the basil. Serve immediately.

Dump and Forget Chicken Cacciatore

This recipe is the second recipe my son learned to cook in the Instant Pot. He was so proud of how it turned out that he took it to work for lunch every day, the entire week. You would think he never had chicken cacciatore in his life. If he could make this, and be as proud as he was, you can do it too!

COOKING TIME: 16 MINUTES — SERVES 4

1 tbsp (15 ml) extra virgin olive oil (EVOO)

1 small onion, roughly chopped

3 cloves garlic, chopped

1 red bell pepper, roughly chopped

1 cup (70 g) sliced white mushrooms

2 cups (360 g) diced tomatoes

1 tsp dried rosemary

1 tsp dried oregano

½ cup (90 g) black olives, cut in half

1 large dried whole bay leaf

1 cup (240 ml) good-quality dry red wine

¼ cup (15 g) chopped fresh parsley, divided

2 lbs (907 g) frozen skin-on, bone-in chicken thighs or breasts

½ tsp sea salt

½ tsp freshly ground black pepper

Turn on the Instant Pot by pressing "Sauté" and set to "More." Insert the inner pot and wait until the panel says "Hot."

Add the olive oil to the inner pot. When the oil is hot, add the onion and garlic. Sauté for 1 minute or until the onion is soft. Add the bell pepper, mushrooms, tomatoes, rosemary, oregano, olives, bay leaf, red wine and parsley (reserve 1 tablespoon [4 g] for garnish). Mix the ingredients together. Add the chicken and coat with the mixture. Add the sea salt and black pepper.

Press "Cancel." Close the lid tightly and move the steam release handle to "Sealing."

Press the "Pressure Cooker/Manual" button and set the timer for 15 minutes on HIGH pressure.

When the timer ends, press "Cancel" and allow the Instant Pot to cool down naturally until the float valve drops down. Open the lid carefully.

Separate the chicken pieces and stir. Remove the bay leaf. Transfer the chicken to a serving platter and spoon the sauce on top. Garnish with the remaining parsley and serve immediately.

SAFETY TIP: *The time for this recipe is for one block of frozen chicken thighs. If you use individually frozen chicken thighs or breasts, set the timer for 10 minutes. Regardless of how long it takes, if you end up with uncooked chicken, put it back into the pot and cook for additional 2 to 5 minutes. The internal temperature for safe-to-eat chicken is 165°F (74°C).*

Simple Chicken Biryani

This classic Indian recipe usually takes hours, including marinating the chicken overnight. But if you forgot to plan a day ahead and all you have is a frozen chicken, just follow these directions for a great dish in almost no time at all. For this recipe, you will have to precook the chicken because the rice takes less time to cook.

COOKING TIME: 20 MINUTES — SERVES 4

1 cup (200 g) basmati rice

3 tbsp (39 g) ghee

1 large onion, sliced

½ tsp cumin seeds

½ tsp fennel seeds

4 whole cloves

4 green cardamom pods, crushed

1 tbsp (9 g) minced garlic

2 tsp (4 g) grated fresh ginger

¼ tsp ground turmeric

2 tsp (5 g) sweet paprika

1 tbsp (8 g) garam masala

½ cup (120 ml) chicken stock

2 lbs (907 g) frozen skinless, boneless chicken thighs

½ tsp chopped saffron strands

½ cup (120 ml) plus 2 tbsp (30 ml) warm water, divided

2 dried whole bay leaves

½ cup (8 g) chopped fresh cilantro, divided

¼ cup (23 g) chopped fresh mint leaves

½ tsp sea salt

½ tsp freshly ground black pepper

Turn on the Instant Pot by pressing "Sauté" and set to "More." Insert the inner pot and wait until the panel says "Hot."

Wash the basmati rice thoroughly and cover with enough water to soak for at least 15 to 30 minutes.

Add ghee to the inner pot. When the ghee is hot, add the onion and sauté for 5 minutes or until it's browned. Add the cumin seeds, fennel seeds, cloves and cardamom pods. Stir. Add the garlic, ginger, turmeric, paprika and garam masala. Stir, then deglaze the bottom of the pot with stock to make sure there are no food particles stuck to the pot. Add the chicken thighs and mix to coat with the spices.

Press "Cancel." Close the lid tightly and move the steam release handle to "Sealing." Press the "Pressure Cooker/Manual" button and set the timer for 10 minutes on HIGH pressure.

Meanwhile, in a small bowl, mix the saffron and 2 tablespoons (30 ml) of warm water. Strain the rice and set aside.

When the timer ends, carefully turn the steam release handle to "Venting," press "Cancel" and allow the Instant Pot to depressurize quickly until the float valve drops down. Open the lid carefully.

Separate the chicken thighs and stir. Add the following in layers in this order: the remaining water, the bay leaves, soaked basmati rice, cilantro (reserve 1 tablespoon [1 g] for garnish), mint leaves, sea salt, black pepper and saffron mixture. Make sure the rice is completely submerged in the liquid and DO NOT mix.

(continued)

Simple Chicken Biryani (continued)

Close the lid tightly and move the steam release handle to "Sealing." Press the "Pressure Cooker/Manual" button and set the timer for 5 minutes on HIGH pressure.

When the timer ends, press "Cancel" and allow the Instant Pot to cool down naturally for 10 minutes. Open the lid carefully and allow the steam to escape. Fluff the rice, remove the bay leaves, separate the chicken pieces and mix. Garnish with the remaining cilantro and serve immediately.

NOTE: *It's important to deglaze the inner pot with stock before adding the chicken and rice so the pot can build pressure. The rice to liquid ratio should be 1:1. If the rice is not completely submerged, add a little bit more water.*

SAFETY TIP: *If the frozen chicken is in one big lump and still too frozen to separate after cooking, put it back into the pot and cook for 5 minutes. The internal temperature of safe-to-eat chicken is 165°F (74°C).*

Easy Peasy Coq au Vin

I have a confession to make. I still don't know how to pronounce "coq au vin" properly, but I did learn that you can't call it "chicken coq au vin" because "coq" means "rooster." I also learned that in some recipes, you could use a whole bottle of good-quality dry red wine to braise it in the oven for a ridiculously long time. But in my easy peasy version, you only need 2 cups (480 ml) of good-quality red wine and frozen chicken! And I know Julia Child is turning over in her grave, NOT because I'm using frozen chicken but because of how good my version tastes "in spite of it all." Or should I say, "because of it all." I think the latter. You decide.

COOKING TIME: 24 MINUTES — SERVES 4

1 lb (454 g) frozen skin-on, bone-in chicken thighs

½ cup (120 ml) water

2 tbsp (30 ml) extra virgin olive oil (EVOO), divided

4 strips of bacon

1 medium onion, sliced

1 tsp minced garlic

1 tsp sea salt

½ tsp freshly ground black pepper

3 medium carrots, diagonally sliced

½ cup (35 g) cremini or white mushrooms, stems removed, thickly sliced

¼ cup (15 g) chopped fresh parsley, divided

1 tsp dried thyme

1 tsp dried tarragon

1 tsp herbes de Provence

½ cup (120 ml) unsalted chicken stock

2 cups (480 ml) good-quality dry red wine, like burgundy

2 tbsp (26 g) unsalted ghee, melted

2 tbsp (16 g) tapioca flour

½ lb (226 g) frozen pearl onions

Turn on the Instant Pot by pressing the "Pressure Cooker/Manual" button and set the timer for 6 minutes on HIGH pressure. Insert the inner pot. Add the chicken and water in the inner pot. Close the lid tightly and move the steam release handle to "Sealing."

When the timer ends, carefully turn the steam release handle to "Venting," press "Cancel" and allow the Instant Pot to depressurize quickly, until the float valve drops down. Open the lid carefully. Transfer the chicken and the broth to a bowl and set aside.

Turn on the Instant Pot by pressing "Sauté" and set to "More." Wipe down the inner pot, insert it in the Instant Pot, and wait until the panel says "Hot."

Add 1 tablespoon (15 ml) of EVOO to the inner pot. When the oil is hot, add the bacon strips and sauté for 3 minutes or until lightly browned. Remove the bacon to a plate with a slotted spoon. Add the remaining EVOO to the inner pot and add the onion, garlic, sea salt and black pepper. Sauté for 1 minute or until the onion is soft. Add the chicken pieces and sauté for 2 minutes or until they are slightly browned. Add the bacon strips, carrots, mushrooms, parsley (reserve 1 tablespoon [4 g] for garnish), thyme, tarragon, herbes de Provence, reserved broth, stock and wine. Stir to incorporate all the ingredients.

Press "Cancel." Close the lid tightly and move the steam release handle to "Sealing." Press the "Pressure Cooker/Manual" button and set the timer for 10 minutes on HIGH pressure.

(continued)

Easy Peasy Coq au Vin (continued)

Meanwhile, combine the melted ghee and tapioca flour to make a roux, and set aside.

When the timer ends, press "Cancel" and allow the Instant Pot to cool down naturally, until the float valve drops down. Open the lid carefully.

Separate the chicken pieces, add the frozen pearl onions and the tapioca roux. Stir to thicken for 2 minutes, deglazing the bottom of the pot occasionally. Transfer the chicken to a serving platter and spoon the sauce on top. Garnish with the remaining parsley and serve immediately.

Nightshade-Free Turkey Curry Chili

This is not your ordinary bland "white chili." The flavor department is kicked up a notch to make up for being nightshade-free. You won't find spicy peppers or red tomatoes, but the savory flavors and hearty vegetables put this chili in a class all by itself. You can make this with either frozen ground turkey or chicken. You are the boss!

COOKING TIME: 9 MINUTES — SERVES 4

½ cup (120 ml) water

1 lb (454 g) frozen ground turkey

2 tbsp (26 g) ghee

½ cup (80 g) diced onion

4 cloves garlic, crushed

2 cups (268 g) diced sweet potatoes

2 cups (140 g) sliced green cabbage

1 medium carrot, diced

1 rib celery, diced

1 cup (70 g) sliced white mushrooms

1 tsp ground cumin

2 tsp (4 g) curry powder

1 tsp sea salt

¼ cup (4 g) chopped fresh cilantro, divided

½ cup (120 ml) unsalted chicken broth

½ tsp freshly ground black pepper

2 large dried whole bay leaves

1 cup (240 ml) coconut cream, divided

1 lime, sliced for garnish

1 avocado, pitted and sliced for garnish

Turn on the Instant Pot by pressing the "Pressure Cooker/Manual" button and set the timer for 3 minutes on HIGH pressure. Insert the inner pot, add the water and ground turkey. Close the lid tightly and move the steam release handle to "Sealing."

When the timer ends, carefully turn the steam release handle to "Venting," press "Cancel" and allow the Instant Pot to depressurize quickly until the float valve drops down. Open the lid carefully.

Using tongs, transfer the turkey to a cutting board and chop it into smaller bite-size pieces with a knife. Reserve the cooking liquid from the inner pot in a small bowl and wipe down the inner pot.

Press "Sauté" and set to "More." Insert the inner pot and wait until the panel says "Hot." Melt the ghee in the inner pot and add the onion and garlic. Sauté for 1 minute or until the onion is soft. Add the turkey, the reserved cooking liquid, sweet potatoes, cabbage, carrot, celery, mushrooms, cumin, curry powder, sea salt, cilantro (reserve 1 tablespoon [1 g] for garnish), broth, black pepper and bay leaves to the inner pot.

Close the lid tightly and move the steam release handle to "Sealing." Press the "Pressure Cooker/Manual" button and set the timer for 5 minutes on HIGH pressure.

When the timer ends, press "Cancel" and allow the Instant Pot to cool down naturally until the float valve drops down. Open the lid carefully.

Add ½ cup (120 ml) coconut cream to the pot and stir. Whisk the remaining coconut cream and set aside. Break up any ground turkey lumps. Ladle the chili into bowls, garnish with the remaining cilantro, whipped coconut cream, lime and avocado. Serve immediately.

Chicken and Apple Patties with Cabbage Hash

Make batches of these patties and freeze them for a quick breakfast. They freeze well, and they cook so quickly in the Instant Pot that it'll save you from skipping breakfast before you rush out the door in the morning.

COOKING TIME: 6 MINUTES — SERVES 4

1 lb (454 g) fresh ground chicken

1 Granny Smith apple, finely diced

1 tbsp (15 ml) maple syrup

¼ tsp sea salt

¼ tsp freshly ground black pepper

2 tbsp (30 ml) extra virgin olive oil (EVOO), divided

2 tbsp (20 g) finely diced onion or shallot

2 cloves garlic

½ small red bell pepper, finely chopped

8 oz (226 g) cabbage, thinly sliced

1 tsp apple cider vinegar

1 tbsp (4 g) finely chopped fresh parsley

To make the chicken and apple patties to freeze, combine the ground chicken, apple, maple syrup, sea salt and black pepper in a medium mixing bowl. Mix well and form 2-inch (5-cm) patties and place them on a sheet pan and freeze. Store them in a ziplock bag in the freezer for up to 1 month.

To cook the patties, turn on the Instant Pot by pressing "Sauté" and set to "More." Insert the inner pot and wait until the panel says "Hot."

Add 1 tablespoon (15 ml) of EVOO to the inner pot. When the oil is hot, add the frozen chicken patties and brown for 1 minute on each side. Transfer the patties to a plate and set aside. Add 1 tablespoon (15 ml) of EVOO to the inner pot and when the oil is hot, add the onion, garlic, bell pepper and cabbage. Sauté for 2 minutes or until the cabbage is soft. Add the apple cider vinegar to the inner pot and deglaze the bottom. Place the chicken patties on top of the cabbage.

Press "Cancel." Close the lid tightly and move the steam release handle to "Sealing." Press the "Pressure Cooker/Manual" button and set the timer for 2 minutes on HIGH pressure.

When the timer ends, carefully turn the steam release handle to "Venting," press "Cancel" and allow the Instant Pot to depressurize quickly, until the float valve drops down. Open the lid carefully.

Place the cabbage and chicken patties on plates, and garnish with the parsley before serving.

NOTE: *Normally, you need at least ½ cup (120 ml) of liquid for the Instant Pot to pressurize. For this recipe, the cabbage and onion will sweat and produce enough liquid. Plus adding apple cider vinegar will also help with the liquid amount. The pot will heat up very quickly and create enough pressure to seal the pot. It will also depressurize quickly, too.*

Moroccan Chicken Tagine

This briny and slightly sweet chicken is famous for taking hours to braise in a special clay vessel called a tagine. But you don't need a fancy Moroccan tagine to make this delicious chicken dish. It's a cinch to make in the Instant Pot without losing its authentic Moroccan flavor.

COOKING TIME: 16 MINUTES — SERVES 4

1 lb (454 g) frozen skin-on, bone-in chicken thighs

½ cup (120 ml) water

2 tbsp (30 ml) extra virgin olive oil (EVOO), divided

1 medium onion, sliced thin

6 cloves garlic, finely chopped or minced

1 tsp grated fresh ginger

½ cup (90 g) pitted Kalamata olives, cut in half

½ cup (90 g) pitted green olives, cut in half

½ cup (89 g) chopped dried Medjool dates

1 tsp sweet paprika

¼ tsp ground cinnamon

½ tsp ground coriander

½ tsp ground cumin

½ tsp ground turmeric

Zest and juice of 1 lemon

½ cup (120 ml) chicken stock

¼ cup (60 ml) good-quality dry white wine

¼ cup (15 g) chopped fresh parsley, divided

Add the chicken thighs and ½ cup (120 ml) of water to the inner pot. Close the lid tightly and move the steam release handle to "Sealing." Turn on the Instant Pot by pressing the "Pressure Cooker/Manual" button and set the timer for 6 minutes on HIGH pressure.

When the timer ends, carefully turn the steam release handle to "Venting," press "Cancel" and allow the Instant Pot to depressurize quickly, until the float valve drops down. Open the lid carefully. Transfer the chicken thighs and the broth to a bowl and set aside.

Press "Sauté" and set to "More." Wipe down the inner pot, put it back in the Instant Pot and wait until the panel says "Hot." Add 1 tablespoon (15 ml) of EVOO to the inner pot. When the oil is hot, add the onion and garlic. Sauté for 1 minute or until the onion is soft. Add the remaining EVOO, ginger, olives, dates, paprika, cinnamon, coriander, cumin, turmeric, lemon zest, lemon juice, stock, white wine and parsley (reserve 1 tablespoon [4 g] for garnish) to the inner pot. Add the chicken pieces and the reserved broth, and stir.

Press "Cancel." Close the lid tightly and move the steam release handle to "Sealing." Then, press the "Pressure Cooker/Manual" button and set the timer for 9 minutes on HIGH pressure. When the timer ends, press "Cancel" and allow the Instant Pot to cool down naturally until the float valve drops down. Open the lid carefully.

Separate the chicken pieces and stir. Transfer the chicken to a serving platter and spoon the sauce on top. Garnish with the remaining parsley and serve immediately.

SAFETY TIP: *If the frozen chicken is in one big lump and is still too frozen to separate after cooking, put it back into the pot and cook for 5 minutes. The internal temperature of safe-to-eat chicken is 165°F (74°C).*

Easy Chicken Garam Masala

Did you know that curry or garam masala is not a whole spice? They are a combination of various spices and everyone makes it slightly different. It's like Italian seasoning or chili powder. While an Indian cook might make his or her own from scratch, for this recipe I suggest you buy a good-quality brand from a local Asian grocery store or well-stocked grocery store.

COOKING TIME: 19 MINUTES — SERVES 4

2 tbsp (30 ml) avocado oil, divided

1 cup (160 g) sliced onion

2 tbsp (12 g) grated fresh ginger

4 cloves garlic, finely minced or pressed

½ cup (75 g) chopped red bell pepper

1 fresh green chili pepper, slit in the middle and seeded

1 tbsp (8 g) red chili powder

1 tsp ground turmeric

1 tsp ground cumin

1 tbsp (8 g) garam masala

2 large chopped tomatoes (about ¾ cup [120 g])

6 tbsp (98 g) tomato paste

¼ cup (4 g) chopped fresh cilantro stems and leaves, divided (reserve 1 tbsp [1 g] of leaves for garnish)

2 lbs (907 g) frozen skin-on, bone-in chicken thighs

1 cup (240 ml) unsalted chicken broth

Sea salt, to taste

Turn on the Instant Pot by pressing "Sauté" and set to "More." Insert the inner pot and wait until the panel says "Hot."

Add 1 tablespoon (15 ml) of avocado oil to the inner pot. When the oil is hot, add the onion, ginger and garlic. Sauté for 2 minutes. Then, add the bell pepper, green chili pepper, chili powder, turmeric, cumin, garam masala, tomatoes, tomato paste, 3 tablespoons (3 g) of cilantro, chicken thighs and broth. Stir well. Make sure all the thighs are coated and the ingredients are submerged in liquid.

Press "Cancel." Close the lid tightly and move the steam release handle to "Sealing." Press the "Pressure Cooker/Manual" button and set the timer for 15 minutes on HIGH pressure.

When the timer ends, press "Cancel" and allow the Instant Pot to cool down naturally, until the float valve drops down. Open the lid carefully.

Separate the chicken pieces and add sea salt, to taste. Press "Sauté" and simmer for 2 minutes. Press "Cancel," transfer the chicken to a serving platter and spoon the sauce on top. Garnish with the remaining cilantro and serve immediately.

Salsa Verde Chicken

Too bad green tomatillos are seasonal fruit and can only be found at a certain time of the year—because they are so good in chilis and sauces. You should buy them when they are in season and freeze them because you will want this chicken dish all year round. The green tomatillos add a fresh, gorgeous green color and a unique flavor that reminds you of a crisp summer day. If you can find queso fresco made with goat's milk, you should add it as it gives a special dimension to this Latin-inspired chicken dish. If you can't find it, then you can add any goat cheese or skip the cheese altogether. It still makes a delicious chicken dish you can have over rice or cauli rice.

COOKING TIME: 22 MINUTES — SERVES 6

5 small green tomatillos, cut in half

1 fresh jalapeño or habanero pepper, seeded and chopped

1 tbsp (5 g) dried oregano

½ cup (8 g) chopped fresh cilantro, divided

5 cloves garlic, crushed

1 medium onion, chopped

½ cup (120 ml) unsalted chicken broth, divided

2 lbs (907 g) frozen boneless and skinless chicken thighs or breasts

1 cup (240 ml) full-fat coconut cream

Turn on the Instant Pot by pressing the "Pressure Cooker/Manual" button and set the timer for 20 minutes on HIGH pressure. Insert the inner pot, add the tomatillos, jalapeño pepper, oregano, cilantro (reserve 2 tablespoons [2 g] for garnish), garlic, onion and broth. Nestle the chicken pieces in between.

Close the lid tightly and move the steam release handle to "Sealing."

When the timer ends, press "Cancel" and allow the Instant Pot to cool down naturally until the float valve drops down. Open the lid carefully.

Remove the chicken and shred it with a fork. Using an immersion blender or a standing blender, purée the sauce. Add the chicken and the sauce back to the inner pot. Press "Sauté," add the coconut cream and stir. Simmer for 2 minutes or until the sauce bubbles.

Press "Cancel," transfer the chicken to a serving platter and spoon the sauce over the chicken. Garnish with the remaining cilantro and serve immediately.

> NOTE: *You can serve this over rice if you can tolerate it or serve it over cauli rice. You can also serve it with gluten-free nachos or in a wrap. The possibilities are endless!*

Sweet and Tangy Chicken Lettuce Wraps

Plain chicken is well, too plain. But not when you add all sorts of goodies on top and wrap it up in buttery lettuce with sweet and tangy sauce. You can adjust the sweetness and make them Keto or low-carb friendly by omitting or reducing the honey.

COOKING TIME: 18 MINUTES — SERVES 4 TO 6

¼ cup (60 ml) freshly squeezed orange juice

¼ cup (60 ml) tamari or coconut aminos

2 tbsp (30 ml) raw honey

1 tbsp (15 ml) mirin or rice vinegar

1 lb (454 g) frozen boneless, skinless chicken thighs

2 tbsp (30 ml) avocado oil

1 cup (160 g) diced onion

1 tbsp (9 g) finely minced or pressed garlic

2 ribs celery, diced

2 carrots, diced

1 tsp grated fresh ginger

½ tsp sea salt

½ tsp freshly ground black pepper

1 tbsp (9 g) orange zest

1 tbsp (8 g) tapioca flour

2 tbsp (30 ml) water

3 scallions chopped, divided

½ tbsp (8 ml) toasted sesame oil

1 tsp white pepper

1 or 2 small heads of bibb, butter or baby romaine lettuce leaves

1 cucumber, julienned

½ cup (58 g) sliced radishes

1 tsp toasted sesame seeds

1 tsp black sesame seeds

Turn on the Instant Pot by pressing the "Pressure Cooker/Manual" button and set the timer for 6 minutes on HIGH pressure. Insert the inner pot and add the orange juice, tamari, raw honey and mirin. Stir. Add the frozen chicken thighs and spoon some of the liquid on top of the chicken.

Close the lid tightly and move the steam release handle to "Sealing."

When the timer ends, carefully turn the steam release handle to "Venting," press "Cancel" and allow the Instant Pot to depressurize quickly until the float valve drops down. Open the lid carefully.

Using tongs, carefully take out the chicken, place it on a cutting board and dice the meat into small pieces. The chicken pieces might be stuck together, but you should be able to cut through them easily. Set the chicken aside. Reserve the cooking liquid in a small bowl.

Press "Sauté" and set to "More." Insert the inner pot and wait until the panel says "Hot." Add the avocado oil to the inner pot and coat the bottom evenly. When the oil is hot, add the onion and sauté for 1 minute or until it is soft. Add the garlic, celery, carrots, ginger, sea salt, black pepper and orange zest. Stir well.

Add the diced chicken pieces and the reserved cooking liquid back to the inner pot and stir. Press the "Pressure Cooker/Manual" button and set the timer for 10 minutes on HIGH pressure.

Meanwhile, mix the tapioca flour and water in a small bowl to make a slurry. Set aside.

(continued)

Sweet and Tangy Chicken Lettuce Wraps (continued)

When the timer ends, press "Cancel" and allow the Instant Pot to cool down naturally for 10 minutes. Then, carefully turn the steam release handle to the "Venting" position for the steam to escape and the float valve to drop down. Press "Cancel," and then "Sauté."

Open the lid carefully and stir in the scallions (reserve 1 tablespoon [3 g] for garnish), toasted sesame oil and white pepper. Add the tapioca slurry to the inner pot while stirring for 1 minute or until the sauce thickens. Press "Cancel," ladle about 1 cup (240 ml) of sauce into a bowl and reserve for serving.

Using a slotted spoon, transfer the chicken onto the lettuce, garnish with scallions, cucumber, radishes and sesame seeds and serve immediately. You can drizzle the reserved sauce, if needed.

Braised Beef Shank with Citrus Gremolata

Beef shanks or soup bones get no respect. But the news must have gotten out that I love to use this cut for braising rather than for soup because the prices have been going up slowly. It is still less expensive than most cuts of meat and I love using the Instant Pot to braise them. The melt-in-your-mouth textures and sweet flavors of bone marrow and the soft collagen from connective tissues taste like a million bucks. The best part? Yes, you guessed it! You can cook them from frozen! You're welcome.

COOKING TIME: 60 MINUTES — SERVES 4

1 sprig of fresh rosemary

1 sprig of fresh thyme

1 large dried whole bay leaf

2 whole cloves

¼ cup (60 ml) extra virgin olive oil (EVOO), divided

4 frozen beef soup bone shanks

1 tsp sea salt

1 tsp black pepper

1 small onion, diced into ½-inch (1-cm) cubes

3 cloves garlic, crushed

1 small carrot, diced into ½-inch (1-cm) cubes

1 rib celery, diced into ½-inch (1-cm) cubes

2 tbsp (32 g) tomato paste

1 cup (240 ml) good-quality dry red wine

1 cup (240 ml) beef stock

2 tbsp (30 ml) Paleo Worcestershire sauce

1 tbsp (9 g) lemon zest

2 tbsp (8 g) chopped fresh parsley

Place the rosemary, thyme, bay leaf and cloves into cheesecloth and secure with kitchen twine to make a bouquet garni.

Turn on the Instant Pot by pressing "Sauté" and set to "More." Insert the inner pot and wait until the panel says "Hot." Add 2 tablespoons (30 ml) of EVOO and when it's hot, brown all sides of the beef shanks as well as you can, about 2 minutes per piece while sprinkling with sea salt and black pepper on each side. Remove the browned shanks and set aside.

Add the remaining EVOO to the inner pot, and add the onion, garlic, carrot and celery. Sauté for 2 minutes or until the onion is soft. Add the tomato paste and mix well. Return the browned shanks to the inner pot, add the bouquet garni, wine, stock and Worcestershire sauce.

Close the lid tightly and move the steam release handle to "Sealing."

Press "Cancel," then the "Pressure Cooker/Manual" button and set the timer for 45 minutes on HIGH pressure.

When the timer ends, press "Cancel" and allow the Instant Pot to cool down naturally until the float valve drops down.

(continued)

Braised Beef Shank with Citrus Gremolata (continued)

Press "Sauté." Open the lid and carefully remove the cooked shanks from the pot and put them on a serving platter. Remove and discard the bouquet garni. Simmer for about 5 minutes and reduce the sauce by half. Press "Cancel."

Pour the reduced sauce from the pot over the shanks. Garnish with lemon zest and parsley, and drizzle each steak with citrus gremolata.

Citrus Gremolata

MAKES ⅓ CUP (ABOUT 45 G)

⅓ cup (20 g) loosely packed fresh parsley stems and leaves

2 cloves garlic, minced

1 tbsp (9 g) lemon zest

1 tbsp (9 g) lime zest

½ tsp sea salt, or to taste

½ tsp freshly ground black pepper, or to taste

Combine the parsley, garlic, lemon zest, lime zest, sea salt and black pepper in a food processor. Pulse a few times until all the ingredients are finely minced but not liquified.

Light and Creamy Chicken Marsala

This is one of our favorite Italian chicken dishes. It's lighter because I don't dredge the chicken pieces—but one ingredient I don't skimp on is the wine. Please make me proud and use only the good-quality Marsala wine from the wine store and not the cheap kind from the "vinegar and oil" section of the supermarket. You will not regret it.

COOKING TIME: 22 MINUTES — SERVES 4

2 tbsp (30 ml) extra virgin olive oil (EVOO), divided

2 lbs (907 g) frozen boneless, skinless chicken thighs

½ tsp sea salt

½ tsp freshly ground black pepper

½ cup (80 g) diced onion

2 cloves garlic, minced

1 cup (70 g) sliced white or cremini mushrooms

½ cup (120 ml) unsalted chicken broth

½ cup (120 ml) good-quality sweet Marsala wine, divided

¼ cup (15 g) chopped fresh parsley, divided

¼ cup (60 ml) full-fat coconut cream

Turn on the Instant Pot by pressing "Sauté" and set to "More." Insert the inner pot and wait until the panel says "Hot."

Add 1 tablespoon (15 ml) of EVOO to the inner pot. When the oil is hot, add the chicken thighs and brown as well as you can for 2 minutes a side. Sprinkle sea salt and black pepper on top of the chicken. Add the remaining EVOO, onion and garlic. Sauté for 1 minute or until the onion is soft. Add the mushrooms, broth, ¼ cup (60 ml) of Marsala wine and parsley (reserve 1 tablespoon [4 g] for garnish).

Press "Cancel." Close the lid tightly and move the steam release handle to "Sealing." Press the "Pressure Cooker/Manual" button and set the timer for 17 minutes on HIGH pressure.

When the timer ends, press "Cancel" and allow the Instant Pot to cool down naturally, until the float valve drops down. Open the lid carefully.

Separate the chicken pieces, add the remaining Marsala wine and the coconut cream. Stir for 2 minutes or until the sauce thickens. Transfer the chicken to a serving platter, garnish with the remaining parsley and serve immediately.

Korean-Style Braised Chicken (*Dak-Bokkeum-Tang*)

This spicy and slightly sweet chicken stew is one of the classic Korean chicken dishes, and it is usually braised on low heat for hours on the stove top. It should be spicy, but you can use sweet paprika if you can't handle heat. If the stew is too spicy after it's finished, add more honey to temper the heat. If you can't tolerate white potatoes, you can substitute with Japanese white sweet potatoes or daikon. We usually eat this over white rice—with all the juicy liquid over the rice. If you don't eat rice, serve with cauli rice or cauli mash with a side of your favorite vegetables.

COOKING TIME: 20 MINUTES — SERVES 6

1 lb (454 g) white potatoes, Japanese white sweet potatoes or daikon

2 carrots

1 medium onion

¼ cup (60 ml) water

2 tbsp (40 g) wheat-free gochujang (Chung Jung One brand), plus more to taste

1 tbsp (4 g) gochugaru or crushed red pepper (or sweet paprika for less heat), plus more to taste

¼ cup (60 ml) tamari

2 tbsp (30 ml) rice wine or good-quality dry white wine or sherry

2 tbsp (30 ml) honey

1 tbsp (9 g) minced garlic

1 tsp grated fresh ginger

1 tbsp (15 ml) sesame oil

1 tsp sea salt, plus more to taste

1 tsp freshly ground black pepper

2 lbs (907 g) frozen skin-on, bone-in chicken thighs or drumsticks

2 scallions, thinly sliced

1 tsp sesame seeds

Cut the potatoes and carrots in similar sizes—about 2-inch (5-cm) cubes—and shave the sharp edges with a knife to make them smooth. This will prevent the vegetables edges from breaking while cooking and ensures they look nice after they are cooked. Quarter the onion and then slice it thick. Set aside the vegetables.

In a small bowl, combine the water, gochujang, gochugaru, tamari, rice wine, honey, garlic, ginger, sesame oil, sea salt and black pepper. Mix well. Taste to see if it needs more gochujang, gochugaru or sea salt to your taste.

Place the chicken thighs and vegetables in the inner pot and pour the sauce on top and mix well. Coat the chicken thighs well.

Close the lid tightly and move the steam release handle to "Sealing."

Turn on the Instant Pot by pressing the "Pressure Cooker/Manual" button and set the timer for 20 minutes on HIGH pressure.

When the timer ends, press "Cancel" and allow the Instant Pot to cool down naturally until the float valve drops down. Open the lid carefully.

Separate the chicken pieces and stir to mix the sauce and the vegetables. Spoon the chicken pieces and the vegetables into shallow bowls. Top with chopped scallions, sprinkle with sesame seeds and serve immediately.

Weeknight Chicken Piccata

Lemon and capers are the most refreshing combination of flavors. This light meal will be everyone's favorite to eat, and it will be your favorite to prepare because there's no panfrying. And the best part is you can easily make this with frozen chicken breasts!

COOKING TIME: 23 MINUTES — SERVES 4

4 frozen skinless, boneless chicken breasts

½ cup (120 ml) water

1 tsp sea salt

1 tbsp (8 g) tapioca flour

1 tbsp (15 ml) extra virgin olive oil (EVOO), plus more if needed

¼ cup (60 ml) fresh lemon juice

¼ cup (60 ml) good-quality dry white wine, divided

1 tbsp (13 g) ghee

½ tsp freshly ground black pepper

1 tbsp (4 g) chopped fresh parsley

Place the chicken breasts, water and sea salt in the inner pot. Close the lid tightly and move the steam release handle to "Sealing." Turn on the Instant Pot by pressing the "Pressure Cooker/Manual" button and set the timer for 6 minutes on HIGH pressure.

When the timer ends, carefully turn the steam release handle to "Venting," press "Cancel" and allow the Instant Pot to depressurize quickly until the float valve drops down. Open the lid carefully.

Take out the chicken breasts, separate the pieces and pat them dry with a paper towel. Reserve the broth in a small bowl. Discard any white scum and wipe down the inner pot. Place the tapioca flour on a plate. Dredge the chicken pieces lightly on both sides and set aside.

Press "Sauté" and set to "More." Insert the inner pot and wait until the panel says "Hot."

Add 1 tablespoon (15 ml) of EVOO to the inner pot. When the oil is hot, brown the chicken breasts for about 1 minute per side or until each side is browned. Continue until all the chicken pieces are done. Add more EVOO, if needed.

Add the lemon juice, 2 tablespoons (30 ml) of wine and deglaze the pot. Add the reserved chicken broth and ghee to the pot. Stir.

Press "Cancel." Close the lid tightly and move the steam release handle to "Sealing." Press the "Pressure Cooker/Manual" button and set the timer for 9 minutes on HIGH pressure.

When the timer ends, press "Cancel" and allow the Instant Pot to cool down naturally until the float valve drops down. Open the lid carefully.

Add the remaining wine to the inner pot, and mix. Transfer the chicken to a serving platter and spoon the sauce on top of the chicken. Sprinkle with black pepper and garnish with parsley before serving.

Thai Green Curry Chicken

Don't let the word "curry" make you think this is a spicy dish. It's not. It's also not that pungent or extra fragrant. Thai curry is totally different from Indian curry; if you're more of a "mild" type, this dish is for you. Thai food is usually sweet, sour, salty and a little spicy, but this is mild. It is a fast but delicious, warm and toasty dish to make you feel, well, warm and fuzzy. Mild and warm. Yeah. Like a cashmere blanket.

COOKING TIME: 15 MINUTES — SERVES 4

2 tbsp (27 g) coconut oil

6 tbsp (90 g) Thai green curry paste (I use Maesri brand.)

1 tbsp (6 g) finely grated fresh ginger

1 lb (454 g) frozen boneless, skinless chicken thighs

½ cup (120 ml) water

½ cup (80 g) diced onion

1 carrot, diced

2 cups (140 g) thinly sliced green cabbage

1 red bell pepper, julienned

2 fresh red chili peppers, seeded and chopped (optional)

1 tsp sea salt

½ tsp ground white pepper

½ cup (120 ml) full-fat coconut milk

½ cup (8 g) chopped fresh cilantro stems and leaves, divided

¼ cup (6 g) chopped fresh Thai basil leaves, divided

2 tbsp (30 ml) fish sauce (I use Red Boat brand)

1 tbsp (9 g) coconut sugar

¼ cup (60 ml) lime juice plus 4 lime wedges for garnish

Turn on the Instant Pot by pressing "Sauté" and set to "More." Insert the inner pot and wait until the panel says "Hot."

Add the coconut oil to the inner pot. When the oil is hot, add the Thai green curry paste and ginger. Sauté to make a paste. Add the chicken thighs and water, and coat the chicken pieces as well as you can.

Press "Cancel." Close the lid tightly and move the steam release handle to "Sealing."

Press the "Pressure Cooker/Manual" button and set the timer for 6 minutes on HIGH pressure.

When the timer ends, press "Cancel" and carefully turn the steam release handle to "Venting." Allow the Instant Pot to depressurize quickly until the float valve drops down. Open the lid carefully.

Separate the chicken pieces. Add the onion, carrot, cabbage, bell pepper, chili peppers (if using), sea salt, white pepper, coconut milk, cilantro (reserve 1 tablespoon [1 g] for garnish), basil (reserve 1 tablespoon [3 g] for garnish), fish sauce and coconut sugar.

Close the lid tightly and move the steam release handle to "Sealing." Press the "Pressure Cooker/Manual" button and set the timer for 9 minutes on HIGH pressure.

When the timer ends, press "Cancel" and allow the Instant Pot to cool down naturally until the float valve drops down. Open the lid carefully.

Separate the chicken pieces and stir. Add lime juice, garnish with the remaining cilantro, basil leaves and the lime wedges, and serve immediately.

Chicken with Cauli Rice

I grew up eating a lot of Latin food in NYC. It was authentic homestyle cooking, like any abuela or tía would cook in their South American kitchens. And their signature dish would be arroz con pollo. Different Latin cultures have different renditions of this classic, but I think any of them would approve this Paleo version of it using the Instant Pot.

COOKING TIME: 18 MINUTES — SERVES 4

2 lbs (907 g) frozen boneless, skinless chicken thighs

½ cup (120 ml) water

¼ tsp saffron threads, chopped

2 tbsp (30 ml) warm water

1 cup (180 g) crushed tomatoes

1 cup (180 g) green olives with pimentos and juice

½ cup (120 ml) chicken stock

1 cup (150 g) diced red bell pepper

½ cup (80 g) diced onion

4 cloves garlic, minced

1½ tsp (1 g) dried oregano

1½ tsp (4 g) sweet paprika

2 tsp (5 g) ground cumin

¼ cup (4 g) chopped fresh cilantro stems and leaves, divided

1 tsp sea salt

1 tsp freshly ground black pepper

2 cups (228 g) frozen cauliflower rice

Place the chicken thighs and water in the inner pot. Close the lid tightly and move the steam release handle to "Sealing." Turn on the Instant Pot by pressing the "Pressure Cooker/Manual" button and set the timer for 6 minutes on HIGH pressure.

Meanwhile, mix the saffron with warm water in a small bowl, and set aside.

When the timer ends, press "Cancel" and carefully turn the steam release handle to "Venting." Allow the Instant Pot to depressurize quickly until the float valve drops down. Open the lid carefully.

Using tongs, transfer the chicken to a cutting board and cut it into 2-inch (5-cm) pieces. Remove the white scum around the pot. Put the chicken pieces back in the inner pot. Add the tomatoes, olives, stock, bell pepper, onion, garlic, oregano, paprika, cumin, cilantro (reserve 1 tablespoon [1 g] for garnish), sea salt and black pepper.

Press the "Pressure Cooker/Manual" button and set the timer for 9 minutes on HIGH pressure.

Meanwhile, run the frozen cauliflower rice under cold running water in a sieve to separate them. Set aside.

When the timer ends, press "Cancel" and allow the Instant Pot to cool down naturally until the float valve drops down. Open the lid carefully.

Add the frozen cauliflower rice to the pot, close the pot with a regular lid (not the pressure cooker lid) for 2 minutes or until the cauli rice is warm. Open the lid and stir. Spoon the chicken and cauli rice into bowls, garnish with the remaining cilantro and serve immediately.

Creamy Chicken with Mushrooms

This creamy chicken dish is inspired by Swedish meatballs, but has added mushrooms and coconut cream for the Paleo crowd. It cooks super quickly with very little prep. Serve over zoodles, gluten-free pasta or rice for a quick weeknight dinner!

COOKING TIME: 13 MINUTES — SERVES 4

¼ cup (52 g) ghee, divided

1 cup (160 g) diced onion

3 cups (210 g) quartered white mushrooms

1 tsp sea salt

1 tsp freshly ground black pepper

¼ tsp ground allspice

¼ tsp ground nutmeg

½ cup (120 ml) good-quality dry white wine, divided

2 lbs (907 g) frozen boneless, skinless chicken thighs

1¼ cups (300 ml) unsalted chicken broth, divided

2 tbsp (18 g) arrowroot powder

½ cup (120 ml) full-fat coconut cream

2 tbsp (30 ml) fresh lemon juice

2 tbsp (8 g) chopped fresh parsley

4 bowls of zoodles, gluten-free pasta or rice

Turn on the Instant Pot by pressing "Sauté" and set to "More." Insert the inner pot and wait until the panel says "Hot."

Add 2 tablespoons (26 g) of ghee to the inner pot. When the ghee is hot, add the onion and mushrooms. Sprinkle with sea salt and black pepper, and sauté for 2 minutes or until the onion is translucent and mushrooms are soft. Add the allspice, nutmeg and ¼ cup (60 ml) of the white wine. Continue to sauté for 1 minute. Add the rest of the ghee and the chicken thighs, and sauté until the chicken is browned. Try to brown all the chicken pieces as much as you can. Add 1 cup (240 ml) of the broth and stir.

Press "Cancel." Close the lid tightly and move the steam release handle to "Sealing."

Press the "Pressure Cooker/Manual" button and set the timer for 10 minutes on HIGH pressure.

Meanwhile, in a small bowl, mix the remaining broth and the arrowroot powder to make the slurry. Set aside.

When the timer ends, press "Cancel" and allow the Instant Pot to cool down naturally until the float valve drops down. Open the lid carefully.

Separate the chicken pieces, add the remaining ghee, wine, coconut cream and lemon juice to the pot and stir. Add the slurry and stir until the sauce is thickened. Close the lid for about 1 minute or so.

Garnish with parsley, and serve over zoodles, gluten-free noodles or rice.

Mediterranean Chicken with Artichokes

One of the best pork chop recipes I've had in my life had olives and spicy pepperoncini. It was briny and spicy, but it was very messy to make on the stove top because it uses a lot of olive oil. So, I wondered how it would taste if I used chicken instead of pork, using the Instant Pot. I think it turned out amazing, if I can say so myself. Not only that, adding artichokes made it even more flavorful!

COOKING TIME: 17 MINUTES — SERVES 5

2 lbs (907 g) frozen boneless, skinless chicken thighs

1 small onion, chopped

2 cloves garlic, crushed

1 bell pepper, seeded and chopped

1 cup (180 g) diced tomatoes

1 cup (180 g) green olives, pitted and sliced, with brine

½ cup (32 g) bottled hot cherry peppers, sliced with liquid

¼ cup (32 g) non-pareil capers with liquid

1 cup (300 g) canned or bottled artichoke hearts

1 tbsp (7 g) Italian seasoning

1 tsp dried oregano

2 tbsp (30 ml) fresh lemon juice

2 tbsp (8 g) chopped fresh parsley, divided

¼ cup (60 ml) good-quality dry white wine

1 tsp sea salt, or to taste

1 tsp freshly ground black pepper

Place the frozen chicken thighs in the inner pot. Add the onion, garlic, bell pepper, tomatoes, olives, cherry peppers, capers, artichoke hearts, Italian seasoning, oregano, lemon juice, 1 tablespoon (4 g) of parsley, white wine, sea salt and black pepper.

Close the lid tightly and move the steam release handle to "Sealing."

Turn on the Instant Pot by pressing the "Pressure Cooker/Manual" button and set the timer for 15 minutes on HIGH pressure.

When the timer ends, press "Cancel" and allow the Instant Pot to cool down naturally until the float valve drops down. Open the lid carefully.

Stir and separate the chicken thighs. Close the lid for 2 minutes and then open the lid.

Place the chicken and vegetables on serving plates. Add more sea salt, if needed. Garnish with the remaining parsley and serve immediately.

Barbacoa for Days

This recipe makes a large batch so it's great for parties or for leftovers. I think it tastes better the next day with all the flavors that get infused and marinated. It freezes well, too, so make a large batch to defrost, reheat and serve when needed. Serve with cauli rice, in a taco or in a burrito bowl. Think of the endless possibilities!

COOKING TIME: 45 MINUTES — SERVES 6 TO 8

2 tbsp (30 ml) extra virgin olive oil (EVOO)

2 lbs (907 g) frozen chuck roast

1 lb (454 g) frozen oxtail bones

1 small onion, chopped

4 cloves garlic, crushed

1 tsp sea salt

1 tsp black pepper

1 cup (240 ml) beef stock

1 tsp ground cumin

½ tsp ground coriander

1 tsp dried oregano

½ tsp ground cinnamon

1 tsp whole cloves

1 (7-oz [198-g]) can chipotle chili peppers in adobo with sauce

1 tbsp (15 ml) apple cider vinegar

1 green bell pepper, chopped

2 dried whole bay leaves

½ cup (8 g) chopped fresh cilantro stems and leaves, divided

Turn on the Instant Pot by pressing "Sauté" and set to "More." Insert the inner pot and wait until the panel says "Hot." Add the EVOO and when it is hot, add the meat in batches, and brown the surfaces for 3 minutes on each side as well as you can. Remove the browned meat and set aside.

Sauté the onion and garlic for 2 minutes or until the onion is soft. Add the meat, sea salt, black pepper, stock, cumin, coriander, oregano, cinnamon, cloves, chipotle peppers and adobo sauce, vinegar, bell pepper, bay leaves and 2 tablespoons (2 g) of cilantro to the inner pot. Close the lid tightly and move the steam release handle to "Sealing."

Press "Cancel," then the "Pressure Cooker/Manual" button and set the timer for 40 minutes on HIGH pressure.

When the timer ends, press "Cancel" and allow the Instant Pot to cool down naturally until the float valve drops down. Open the lid carefully.

Debone the oxtail bones, remove the bay leaves and shred the chuck roast. Put the meat back in the pot and stir. You can serve immediately with the remaining cilantro as a garnish, or marinate the beef in the sauce overnight and serve a day later for more flavor.

Chipotle Chili con Carne

Chili has many origins, but Texas is the gateway to American chili. Chili was a staple throughout the big cattle drives around the state, but it used to be served alongside beans. And the cowboys used to mix them up together and at some point, bean chili became popular. But if you're on the Paleo diet, you want to eat as close to the original food as you can—so chili should not include beans. Not to mention, beans have anti-nutrients, phytates and lectins. Having said that, I think the original version with only meat in the chili is tastier anyway. Why go with fillers when you can just go for the real ingredient: beef!

COOKING TIME: 18 MINUTES — SERVES 6

2 tbsp (30 ml) extra virgin olive oil (EVOO), divided

2 lbs (907 g) frozen stew meat, cut into 2-inch (5-cm) cubes

1 cup (160 g) chopped onion

6 cloves garlic, chopped

1 (12-oz [340-g]) can chipotle peppers in adobo

½ cup (120 ml) beef stock

15 oz (425 g) fresh or canned crushed tomatoes

½ cup (120 ml) good-quality dry red wine

1 tbsp (7 g) ground cumin

2 tbsp (16 g) chili powder

1 tsp garlic powder

1 tsp dried oregano

½ cup (8 g) chopped fresh cilantro, divided

1 fresh jalapeño pepper, sliced

½ cup (120 ml) coconut cream, whipped

Turn on the Instant Pot by pressing "Sauté" and set to "More." Insert the inner pot and wait until the panel says "Hot."

Add 1 tablespoon (15 ml) of EVOO to the inner pot, and when the oil is hot, carefully add the frozen stew meat pieces and brown for about 2 minutes total.

Add the remaining EVOO to the inner pot. When the oil is hot, add the onion and garlic. Sauté for 1 minute or until the onion is soft. Add the chipotle peppers and adobo sauce, stock, tomatoes, red wine, cumin, chili powder, garlic powder, oregano and cilantro (reserve 1 tablespoon [1 g] for garnish). Stir to mix.

Close the lid tightly and move the steam release handle to "Sealing."

Press "Cancel," then the "Pressure Cooker/Manual" button and set the timer for 15 minutes on HIGH pressure.

When the timer ends, press "Cancel" and allow the Instant Pot to cool down naturally until the float valve drops down. Open the lid carefully.

Ladle the chili into bowls and garnish with the whipped coconut cream, remaining cilantro and jalapeño pepper before serving.

NOTE: *If the stew meat pieces are frozen together, put them under cold water and separate the pieces before adding them to the pot.*

Ropa Vieja with Cauli Rice

Skirt steak is so undervalued and underrated that I love using it as often as possible. Because it's not overly fatty, it's great to use the Instant Pot to make the meat more tender and packed with flavor. If you remember to marinate the meat, it's even better—but regardless of whether you remembered to do that or not, this recipe is still one of my favorite recipes to make from frozen.

COOKING TIME: 30 MINUTES — SERVES 4

2 tbsp (30 ml) extra virgin olive oil (EVOO), divided

1 cup (160 g) diced onion

6 cloves garlic, minced

1 green bell pepper, diced

2 lbs (907 g) frozen skirt steak

1 tsp sea salt

½ tsp freshly ground black pepper

1 tsp ground cumin

1 tsp cayenne pepper

2 tbsp (30 ml) lime juice

2 fresh jalapeño peppers, sliced, divided

1 tbsp (5 g) dried oregano

2 dried whole bay leaves

1 cup (240 ml) tomato sauce

8 oz (226 g) tomato paste

1 cup (240 ml) beef stock

½ cup (8 g) chopped fresh cilantro, divided

1 head of cauliflower or 4 cups (456 g) frozen cauliflower rice

Turn on the Instant Pot by pressing "Sauté" and set to "More." Insert the inner pot and wait until the panel says "Hot."

Add 1 tablespoon (15 ml) of EVOO to the inner pot. When the oil is hot, add the onion and garlic. Sauté for 1 minute or until the onion is soft. Add the remaining oil and bell pepper, and sauté for 1 minute. Add the frozen skirt steak, sea salt, black pepper, cumin, cayenne pepper, lime juice, 1 jalapeño pepper, oregano, bay leaves, tomato sauce, tomato paste, stock and cilantro (reserve 1 tablespoon [1 g] for garnish). Mix well.

Press "Cancel." Close the lid tightly and move the steam release handle to "Sealing." Press the "Pressure Cooker/Manual" button and set the timer for 25 minutes on HIGH pressure.

Meanwhile, prepare the cauli rice by grating the cauliflower florets on a cheese grater. Place the grated cauliflower in an ovenproof bowl that can fit in the Instant Pot. Or you can microwave the cauli rice. I prefer cooking it in the Instant Pot.

When the timer ends, press "Cancel" and allow the Instant Pot to cool down naturally until the float valve drops down. Open the lid carefully.

Remove the bay leaves and shred the meat in the pot and stir. Put a trivet in the pot. Place the bowl with grated cauliflower on the trivet. Close the lid but don't lock it tight and bring to gentle simmer on "Sauté" for 3 minutes. Take out the cauliflower and the trivet. Plate the meat and cauliflower rice, garnish with the remaining jalapeño pepper slices, remaining cilantro and serve immediately.

Swedish Meatballs over Cauliflower and Parsnip Purée

This is one of our favorite appetizers, and the meatballs also make a great meal over noodles or mashed potatoes. But serve them with cauli mash instead and no one will even know the difference. Make a huge batch and freeze them for a quick weeknight meal.

COOKING TIME: 20 MINUTES — SERVES 4

MEATBALLS

1 lb (454 g) ground beef

½ cup (80 g) finely diced onion

2 tbsp (8 g) chopped fresh parsley

1 large egg, beaten

2 tbsp (18 g) minced garlic

1 tsp sea salt

1 tsp black pepper

¼ tsp ground nutmeg

¼ tsp ground allspice

1 tbsp (8 g) tapioca flour

COOKING THE MEATBALLS

2 tbsp (26 g) ghee

½ cup (80 g) diced onion

1 cup (240 ml) beef stock

1 tbsp (8 g) tapioca flour, plus more if needed

½ cup (120 ml) full-fat coconut cream

¼ tsp sea salt

¼ tsp white pepper

2 tbsp (30 ml) apple cider vinegar

¼ tsp ground nutmeg

2 tbsp (8 g) chopped fresh parsley, divided

Cauliflower and Parsnip Purée (page 178)

To make the meatballs to freeze, in a medium-sized mixing bowl, combine the ground beef, onion, parsley, egg, garlic, sea salt, black pepper, nutmeg, allspice and tapioca flour. Mix well. Form 1- to 1½-inch (2.5- to 3.5-cm) balls and freeze them in a single layer on a sheet pan. When they are completely frozen, you can store them in a ziplock freezer bag for up to 1 month. You can even double the recipe to freeze for later.

To cook the meatballs, turn on the Instant Pot by pressing "Sauté" and set to "More." Insert the inner pot and wait until the panel says "Hot." Melt the ghee in the inner pot, add the onion and sauté. Brown the meatballs, a few at a time until all of them are done. The oil will splatter so be careful when placing them in the inner pot. This should take about 3 minutes. When they are all browned, add them back to the inner pot and add the stock.

Close the lid tightly and move the steam release handle to "Sealing." Press "Cancel," then the "Pressure Cooker/Manual" button and set the timer for 15 minutes on HIGH pressure.

When the timer ends, press "Cancel" and allow the Instant Pot to cool down naturally until the float valve drops down.

Press "Sauté" and open the lid. Add the tapioca flour, coconut cream, sea salt, white pepper, apple cider vinegar, ground nutmeg, and 1 tablespoon (4 g) of parsley to the pot. Stir for 2 minutes or until the sauce bubbles and thickens. If you like thicker sauce, add more tapioca flour and stir. Press "Cancel." Transfer the meatballs with sauce to plates with the purée. Garnish with the remaining parsley and serve immediately.

Adult Sloppy Joes with a Kick

The sloppy Joe flavors are simple, but this version is nothing you ever had as a kid. If you're making this for your children, you can reduce the amount of the red pepper and use beef stock instead of beer. The sweet potatoes are perfect for stuffing and loading them up with this goodness.

COOKING TIME: 23 MINUTES — SERVES 4

1 lb (454 g) frozen ground beef

1 tbsp (15 ml) avocado oil

½ cup (80 g) diced onion

1 large red bell pepper, diced

3 cloves garlic, minced

½ tsp sea salt

1 tsp freshly ground black pepper

½ tsp dried thyme

2 tsp (2 g) crushed red pepper flakes

½ cup (120 ml) ketchup

1 tsp Dijon mustard

2 tsp (6 g) coconut sugar

1 cup (240 ml) tomato sauce

2 tsp (10 g) tomato paste

1 tbsp (15 ml) Paleo Worcestershire sauce

½ cup (120 ml) gluten-free beer (beef stock if serving to children)

4 medium sweet potatoes, washed and dried

2 tbsp (15 g) tapioca flour

1 scallion, chopped

Take out the frozen ground beef from the freezer and remove from the package onto an aluminum sheet pan.

Turn on the Instant Pot by pressing "Sauté" and set to "More." Insert the inner pot and wait until the panel says "Hot." Add the avocado oil in the inner pot and wait until the oil is hot and smoking. Add the onion, bell pepper and garlic. Sauté for 3 minutes or until the onion and bell pepper become a little soft.

Add the ground beef to the inner pot and brown both sides as well as you can until the color changes to an opaque brown. Add the sea salt, black pepper, thyme, crushed red pepper, ketchup, Dijon mustard, coconut sugar, tomato sauce, tomato paste, Worcestershire sauce and beer to the inner pot. Stir to combine all of the ingredients as well as you can and ladle some of the ingredients on top of the ground beef.

Place a trivet inside and place 4 sweet potatoes on top. Close the lid tightly and move the steam release handle to "Sealing." Press "Cancel," then the "Pressure Cooker/Manual" button and set the timer for 10 minutes on HIGH pressure.

When the timer ends, press "Cancel" and move the steam release handle to "Venting." Open the lid carefully.

Using tongs, place the sweet potatoes on a platter and set aside. Remove the trivet. Take a spatula and break up the ground beef into small pieces. Add the tapioca flour and mix well into the sauce. Simmer for 10 minutes or until the sauce thickens.

Cut the sweet potatoes in halves, scoop about ½ cup (60 ml) of sloppy Joe on top of each half, garnish with scallion and serve immediately.

Boneless Rib Eye Steak with Rosemary and Garlic Butter

When I wrote the book Keto Cooking with Your Instant Pot®, *I was pleasantly surprised to discover how easy it is to cook a prime rib in the Instant Pot. Well, I took the same technique to make a perfect rib eye steak in the Instant Pot from frozen—you know, for that night when you forget to defrost your steaks! You can easily finish the steaks in the Instant Pot by following the instructions here or you can broil them in the oven to cut down the time even more. Either way, don't fret when you forget to take out the meat from the freezer! It may turn out to be your favorite way to cook steaks!*

COOKING TIME: 5 MINUTES — SERVES 4

4 (10 oz [283 g]) frozen rib eye steaks, about 1-inch (2.5-cm) thick

4 tsp (24 g) sea salt

2 tsp (4 g) freshly ground black pepper

2 tbsp (26 g) ghee, divided

4 sprigs of fresh rosemary

8 large cloves garlic, crushed

Take out the frozen steaks and run them under cold water to rinse off any frozen blood on the outside. Dry them with a paper towel and place them on a tray in a single layer.

Place ¾ cup (180 ml) of water in the inner pot and place the trivet inside. Put the 4 steak pieces, standing on their sides, on the trivet. Don't stack them on top of each other. Close the lid tightly and move the steam release handle to "Sealing." Turn on the Instant Pot by pressing the "Pressure Cooker/Manual" button and set the timer for 3 minutes on HIGH pressure.

When the timer ends, allow the Instant Pot to cool down naturally until the float valve drops down. This should take about 5 minutes. If the valve doesn't drop down after 5 minutes, carefully turn the steam release handle to "Venting" position for the steam to escape and the float valve to drop down. Press "Cancel," then press "Sauté" and set to "More."

Transfer the steaks to a platter, remove the trivet, pour out the water and wipe down the inner pot. Take the core temperature of the steak and make sure it's cooked to your liking. Core temperature out of the Instant Pot should be 140°F (60°C) for medium-rare, 155°F (68°C) for medium and 165°F (74°C) for well-done. The final temperature should rise 5°F (6°C) after it rests. Sprinkle ½ teaspoon of sea salt and ¼ teaspoon of black pepper on each side of the steaks.

(continued)

Boneless Rib Eye Steak with Rosemary and Garlic Butter (continued)

If you are using the Instant Pot to finish the steaks, wait until the panel says "Hot." Then, add 1 tablespoon (13 g) of ghee in the inner pot and coat the bottom evenly. Sauté each steak for 2 minutes per side or until both sides are brown. Add 1 sprig of rosemary and 2 cloves of garlic per steak and sauté while the steaks are getting browned. Repeat for the other three steaks, adding more rosemary, garlic and ghee as necessary. When all the steaks are done, let them rest for 5 minutes.

Serve while steaks are hot with vegetables of your choice.

To finish the steaks in the oven, turn on the oven to "Broil." Place the steaks on a broiler pan and place the pan about 4 to 6 inches (10 to 15 cm) under the broiler. Cook for 1 minute or until one side is browned. Turn the steaks over and brown the other side for another minute. Take the steaks out as soon as they are brown and let them rest for 5 minutes. While the steaks are resting, sauté all the rosemary and garlic with ghee in the Instant Pot. Drizzle the rosemary and garlic butter on top of the steaks before serving with vegetables of your choice.

Beef Taco Salad with Plantain Chips

Every day should be Taco Tuesday, don't you think? And if you are a salad lover, taco salad should be served with every meal. I think it's even better than plain tacos—because who has the time to prep all the toppings and put them in bazillion bowls on the table for people to pick? Prepare the salad before serving and things go much more smoothly at dinner time.

COOKING TIME: 20 MINUTES — SERVES 4

PLANTAIN CHIPS

2 green plantains, peeled and sliced ⅛-inch (3-mm) thick

1 tbsp (15 ml) extra virgin olive oil (EVOO)

1 tsp sea salt

½ tsp ground cumin

TACO MEAT

1 lb (454 g) frozen ground beef

½ cup (120 ml) water

½ cup (80 g) diced onion

4 cloves garlic, minced

1 lb (454 g) diced tomatoes

¼ cup (4 g) chopped fresh cilantro, divided

TACO SEASONING

1 tsp chili powder

½ tsp sweet paprika

1 tsp ground cumin

½ tsp garlic powder

½ tsp onion powder

1 tsp sea salt

SALAD

1 head iceberg lettuce, thinly sliced

2 avocados, sliced

2 fresh jalapeño peppers, thinly sliced

1 small red onion, thinly sliced

1 cup (180 g) black olives, halved (optional)

To make the plantain chips, preheat the oven to 400°F (200°C, or gas mark 6). Place the plantain slices in a medium-sized mixing bowl and toss with the EVOO, sea salt and cumin. Put the plantain pieces in a single layer on a sheet pan. Turn them over at half way and bake until both sides are crispy and browned. This may take up to 15 to 20 minutes total.

To make the taco meat, add the frozen ground beef and water to the inner pot. Close the lid tightly and move the steam release handle to "Sealing." Turn on the Instant Pot by pressing the "Pressure Cooker/Manual" button and set the timer for 3 minutes on HIGH pressure.

When the timer ends, carefully turn the steam release handle to "Venting," press "Cancel" and allow the Instant Pot to depressurize quickly until the float valve drops down. Open the lid carefully.

To make the taco seasoning, in a small bowl, mix together the chili powder, paprika, cumin, garlic powder, onion powder and sea salt. Set aside.

(continued)

Beef Taco Salad with Plantain Chips (continued)

Transfer the meat to a cutting board and keep the liquid in the inner pot. Chop the meat into smaller pieces with a knife. The meat might not be totally defrosted but you should be able to cut through with a sharp knife. Place the chopped beef back into the inner pot and add the onion, garlic, tomatoes, cilantro (reserve 1 tablespoon [1 g] for garnish) and 1 tablespoon (15 g) taco seasoning. Stir to break up the meat some more.

Close the lid tightly and move the steam release handle to "Sealing." Turn on the Instant Pot by pressing the "Pressure Cooker/Manual" button and set the timer for 3 minutes on HIGH pressure.

Meanwhile, wash the vegetables and place the lettuce in 4 salad bowls. If the plantain chips are done, turn off the oven and take out the sheet pan to cool.

When the timer ends, press "Cancel" and allow the Instant Pot to cool down naturally until the float valve drops down. Open the lid carefully.

Stir to mix the ingredients. With a slotted spoon, divide the taco meat to the 4 prepped salad bowls. Add the avocados, jalapeño peppers, red onion and olives (if using). Drizzle the liquid from the inner pot, and garnish with the remaining cilantro. Serve immediately with plantain chips.

NOTE: *Make double batches of taco seasoning in advance. Store in an airtight container in a dark cabinet for up to 1 month.*

Korean Beef Donburi with Rice

My son can finish off 2 pounds (908 g) of Bulgogi—a thinly sliced rib eye cut of beef, marinated in a sweet briny Korean-style sauce, wrapped in lettuce leaves with ssamjang, (Korean miso and gochujang sauce)— without blinking an eye. That's enough meat to feed a family of four. So, I developed this quick and easy recipe for those nights when 1.) I don't have thinly sliced rib eye cut of meat or 2.) I forgot to defrost the meat. Either case is common in my house. Make this recipe to have in a lettuce wrap or on a bowl of piping hot rice (if you can tolerate it) or as a part of bibimbap with veggies. You can't go wrong with this umami-filled beef dish that put the Korean cuisine on the gastronomic map. Just ask my son.

COOKING TIME: 17 MINUTES — SERVES 4

½ cup (120 ml) **tamari or coconut aminos**

1 tbsp (15 ml) **blackstrap molasses**

1 tbsp (15 ml) **raw honey**

1 tsp **minced garlic**

1 tsp **grated fresh ginger**

2 tsp (10 ml) **sesame oil, divided**

1 tsp **fish sauce**

1 tsp **sea salt**

1 tsp **freshly ground black pepper**

1 lb (454 g) **frozen ground beef**

½ cup (80 g) **diced onion**

½ cup (64 g) **diced carrots**

1 tsp **mirin (optional)**

¼ cup (12 g) **chopped scallions**

1 tsp **sesame seeds**

4 bowls of **cooked rice or cauli rice**

NOTE: *Double the recipe and freeze it for later. It reheats in the Instant Pot for an even quicker meal.*

In a small mixing bowl, combine the tamari, molasses and honey with a whisk. Add the garlic, ginger, 1 teaspoon of sesame oil, fish sauce, sea salt and black pepper to the bowl. Mix and set aside.

Turn on the Instant Pot by pressing "Sauté" and set to "More." Insert the inner pot and wait until the panel says "Hot." Add the frozen ground beef to the inner pot and let one side brown for 1 minute. Add the onion, carrots and the tamari mixture to the inner pot and stir the liquid and the vegetables for about 1 minute. Then, turn over the ground beef to brown the other side and place the beef on top of the vegetables.

Hit "Cancel." Close the lid tightly and move the steam release handle to "Sealing." Press the "Pressure Cooker/Manual" button and set the timer for 15 minutes on HIGH pressure.

When the timer ends, press "Cancel" and allow the Instant Pot to cool down naturally until the float valve drops down. Open the lid carefully.

Transfer the meat to a cutting board and cut into small pieces with a sharp knife. Put the meat back in the inner pot and mix with the vegetables. Add the remaining sesame oil and mirin (if using). Stir for about 2 minutes. Transfer the meat with vegetables into bowls with rice or cauli rice. Garnish with scallions and sesame seeds before serving.

Everyone's Favorite Beef Teriyaki with Mushrooms

Teriyaki sauce goes well with any type of protein, including fish and vegetables. But beef is everyone's favorite, and you can make this classic dish even if you forgot to defrost the meat!

COOKING TIME: 7 MINUTES — SERVES 4

1 lb (454 g) frozen sirloin or NY strip steak

½ cup (120 ml) beef stock

¼ cup (60 ml) rice vinegar or apple cider vinegar

½ cup (120 ml) tamari or ¾ cup (180 ml) coconut aminos

1 tsp fresh grated ginger

2 cloves garlic, pressed or finely minced

2 tbsp (30 ml) raw honey

1 tbsp (15 ml) blackstrap molasses

1 tsp ground ginger

1 tsp garlic powder

2 cups (284 g) mushrooms, sliced

2 tsp (6 g) sesame seeds, divided

1 tbsp (9 g) arrowroot powder

2 tbsp (30 ml) cold water

1 tsp sesame oil

¼ cup (12 g) chopped scallions

Add the meat and stock to the inner pot. Close the lid tightly and move the steam release handle to "Sealing." Turn on the Instant Pot by pressing the "Pressure Cooker/Manual" button and set the timer for 2 minutes on HIGH pressure.

Meanwhile, make the teriyaki seasoning in a small bowl. Combine the vinegar, tamari, grated ginger, garlic, honey, molasses, ground ginger, garlic powder, mushrooms and 1 teaspoon of sesame seeds. Mix and set aside.

In another small bowl, mix the arrowroot powder and water to make a slurry. Set aside.

When the timer ends, carefully turn the steam release handle to "Venting," press "Cancel," and allow the Instant Pot to depressurize quickly until the float valve drops down. Open the lid carefully.

Using tongs, transfer the meat to a cutting board and slice ¼-inch (6-mm)-thick pieces with a knife. The meat won't be totally defrosted at this point, but you should be able to cut through it with a sharp knife.

Put the meat and the seasoning mixture in the inner pot and close the lid tightly. Move the steam release handle to "Sealing." Press the "Pressure Cooker/Manual" button and set the timer for 3 minutes on HIGH pressure.

When the timer ends, press "Cancel" and allow the Instant Pot to cool down naturally until the float valve drops down. Open the lid carefully.

Add the sesame oil and the arrowroot slurry to the inner pot. Stir for 2 minutes or until the sauce thickens. Garnish with the remaining sesame seeds and scallions, and serve immediately.

NOTE: *You can also use two 8-ounce (226-g) steaks or flank steak and cut across the grain.*

Korean-Style Braised Oxtail

Oxtails are one of the most collagen-rich parts of the cow. They used to be cheaper than other cuts, but now people have caught on and prices have gone up a bit. We love this style of braised oxtail because . . . soy sauce. So, if you like Korean-style beef marinade, you will love this collagen-rich dish.

COOKING TIME: 60 MINUTES — SERVES 6

2 lbs (907 g) frozen oxtail bones

2 cups (480 ml) water

¼ cup (60 ml) sake or good-quality dry white wine

1 tbsp (15 ml) honey

¾ cup (180 ml) tamari

4 cloves garlic, crushed

4 scallions, cut in ½-inch (1-cm) lengths (reserve 1 scallion finely chopped, for garnish)

1 tsp freshly ground black pepper

1 (1-inch [2.5-cm]) piece of fresh ginger, peeled and sliced

1 medium onion, sliced thick

2 carrots, cut into 1-inch (2.5-cm) lengths

3 shiitake mushrooms, sliced thick

2 parsnips, cut in 2-inch (5-cm) cubes

2 tbsp (30 ml) sesame oil, divided

2 tbsp (18 g) toasted sesame seeds, divided

1 tbsp (9 g) black sesame seeds, for garnish

Wash and rinse the frozen oxtail bones and try to separate the pieces. Place the oxtail bones in the inner pot. In a small bowl, mix the water, sake, honey and tamari. Add the liquid mixture over the oxtail bones. Place the garlic, 3 scallions, black pepper, ginger, onion, carrots, mushrooms, parsnips, 1 tablespoon (15 ml) of sesame oil and 1 tablespoon (9 g) toasted sesame seeds around the oxtail bones and on top.

Close the lid tightly and move the steam release handle to "Sealing." Turn on the Instant Pot by pressing the "Pressure Cooker/Manual" button and set the timer for 60 minutes on HIGH pressure.

When the timer ends, press "Cancel" and allow the Instant Pot to cool down naturally until the float valve drops down. Open the lid carefully.

Ladle the stew into bowls. Garnish with chopped scallions, remaining toasted sesame seeds and black sesame seeds. Serve immediately.

NOTE: *To get more flavor from the vegetables, I add all the vegetables in the beginning, but the texture is soft. If you like more texture, you can divide the vegetables and add half of them in the beginning and add the rest after 30 minutes. Do a quick release of the pressure by moving the release handle to "Venting" after 30 minutes. Open the lid, add the vegetables and cook 30 minutes more. Make sure to release the pressure naturally at the end of the cooking cycle.*

Weeknight Pork Tenderloin with Parsnip and Carrots

I'll be honest: How well this dish turned out was a total surprise to me. I knew fresh pork tenderloin was amazing in the Instant Pot, but when the frozen tenderloin came out just as tender, I thought it was a fluke. So, I had to retry the recipe. And I retried it again and again. Each time, the meat came out so tender that my family now asks for this recipe over chicken. Pork is fairly inexpensive, but I stock up on tenderloins if they're ever on sale, just to make this when I'm in a pinch. Remember to cut the long tenderloin shorter than 8 inches (21 cm) before freezing it because that's the diameter of the 6-quart (6-L) inner pot and you want to be sure everything fits.

COOKING TIME: 6 MINUTES — SERVES 4

2 tbsp (26 g) ghee

1 large Vidalia onion, sliced

2 Granny Smith apples, peeled, cored and diced

2 cloves garlic, crushed

2 carrots, cut into 2-inch (5-cm) pieces

2 parsnips, cut into 2-inch (5-cm) pieces

2 lbs (907 g) frozen pork tenderloin, cut in 7-inch (18-cm) length

2 tsp (12 g) sea salt, divided

1 tsp dried thyme

1 tsp dried rosemary

½ cup (120 ml) chicken stock

¼ cup (15 g) chopped fresh parsley, divided

Turn on the Instant Pot by pressing "Sauté" and set to "More." Insert the inner pot and wait until the panel says "Hot."

Add ghee to the inner pot. When the ghee is hot, add the onion, apples and garlic. Sauté for 2 minutes or until the onion is soft. Add the carrots and parsnips to the inner pot and stir. Nestle the pork tenderloin on top of the vegetables, sprinkle 1 teaspoon of sea salt on top of the pork, and add thyme, rosemary, stock and 2 tablespoons (8 g) of parsley to the inner pot.

Press "Cancel." Close the lid tightly and move the steam release handle to "Sealing." Press the "Pressure Cooker/Manual" button and set the timer for 4 minutes on HIGH pressure.

When the timer ends, press "Cancel" and allow the Instant Pot to cool down naturally until the float valve drops down. Open the lid carefully.

Take the internal temperature of the pork to make sure it's 145°F (63°C) in the center of the tenderloin. If it's not, cook for 2 minutes. If the pork is cooked properly, transfer the pork to a cutting board and slice ¼- to ½-inch (6- to 13-mm) thick. Transfer the slices to plates for serving.

With a slotted spoon, transfer the vegetables from the inner pot to the plates. Garnish with the remaining parsley and serve immediately.

Paleo Mapo "Tofu"

My mother-in-law makes the best mapo tofu so I've got the technique down, but I had to omit tofu and peas to Paleotize it for my family. I substitute the tofu with green cabbage and the peas with broccoli and they don't even miss the original version. And this saucy dish is one of our favorite quick meals. You can serve it with rice or substitute cauli rice if you can't tolerate rice.

COOKING TIME: 18 MINUTES — SERVES 4

1 lb (454 g) frozen ground pork

½ cup (120 ml) water

2 tbsp (30 ml) avocado oil

1 medium onion, diced

3 cloves garlic, minced

2 cups (140 g) finely chopped green cabbage

2 carrots, diced

1 cup (156 g) chopped broccoli florets and stem

½ cup (120 ml) tamari

1 tsp fish sauce (I like Red Boat brand)

¼ cup (60 ml) Sriracha hot pepper sauce or 1 tbsp (4 g) crushed red pepper flakes

1 tbsp (9 g) arrowroot powder

2 tbsp (30 ml) water

2 tbsp (30 ml) sesame oil

¼ cup (12 g) chopped scallions

¼ cup (4 g) chopped fresh cilantro stems and leaves

Add the ground pork and water to the inner pot. Close the lid tightly and move the steam release handle to "Sealing." Turn on the Instant Pot by pressing the "Pressure Cooker/Manual" button and set the timer for 6 minutes on HIGH pressure.

When the timer ends, carefully turn the steam release handle to "Venting," press "Cancel" and allow the Instant Pot to depressurize quickly until the float valve drops down. Open the lid carefully.

Using tongs, transfer the meat to a cutting board and cut it into small pieces with a knife. Set aside. Discard the water from the inner pot and wipe away any scum around the pot.

Press "Sauté" and set to "More." Insert the inner pot and wait until the panel says "Hot."

Add the avocado oil to the inner pot. When the oil is hot, add the onion and garlic. Sauté for 1 minute or until the onion is soft. Then, add the cabbage, carrots and broccoli and sauté for 1 minute. Add the pork, tamari, fish sauce and Sriracha to the inner pot and stir.

Press "Cancel." Close the lid tightly and move the steam release handle to "Sealing." Press the "Pressure Cooker/Manual" button and set the timer for 10 minutes on HIGH pressure.

Meanwhile, in a small bowl mix the arrowroot powder and water to make a slurry. Set aside.

When the timer ends, press "Cancel" and allow the Instant Pot to cool down naturally until the float valve drops down. Open the lid carefully.

Mix well and break up any clumps of meat. Add the arrowroot slurry mixture, drizzle with sesame oil and stir. Garnish with scallions and cilantro before serving.

Dim Sum–Style Pork Riblets

We love going to Chinese dim sum restaurants where you can pick just a "few" things you want to eat as the carts filled with yummy Chinese food roll by. And one of the things we love to eat are pork riblets that are flavored with Chinese five-spice powder. They don't need any additional sauces to dip in and they're really addicting. So, when you see riblets at the grocery store, grab them and make these. You will love them!

COOKING TIME: 16 MINUTES — SERVES 4

2 lbs (907 g) frozen pork riblets

½ cup (120 ml) water

1 tbsp (15 ml) tamari

2 tbsp (30 ml) apple cider vinegar

2 tbsp (30 ml) blackstrap unsulphured molasses

½ tsp Chinese five-spice powder

1 tbsp (8 g) garlic powder

1 tbsp (5 g) ground ginger

½ tsp toasted sesame oil

2 tbsp (30 ml) raw honey

½ tsp sea salt

½ tsp freshly ground black pepper

¼ cup (12 g) finely chopped fresh chives or scallions

Add the pork riblets and ½ cup (120 ml) water to the inner pot. Close the lid tightly and move the steam release handle to "Sealing." Turn on the Instant Pot by pressing the "Pressure Cooker/Manual" button and set the timer for 1 minute on HIGH pressure.

When the timer ends, carefully turn the steam release handle to "Venting," press "Cancel," and allow the Instant Pot to depressurize quickly until the float valve drops down. Open the lid carefully.

Using tongs, transfer the pork riblets to a cutting board. Cut in between the ribs and set the riblets aside.

In the inner pot, add the pork riblets, tamari, vinegar, molasses, Chinese five-spice powder, garlic powder, ginger, sesame oil, honey, sea salt and black pepper. Mix to combine.

Close the lid tightly and move the steam release handle to "Sealing." Turn on the Instant Pot by pressing the "Pressure Cooker/Manual" button and set the timer for 15 minutes on HIGH pressure.

When the timer ends, press "Cancel" and allow the Instant Pot to cool down naturally until the float valve drops down. Open the lid carefully.

Garnish with chives or scallions, and serve immediately.

Carefree Carnitas Salad

Carnitas is a popular dish for many reasons, but using it in salads is my favorite. It's a bit crunchy and has so much flavor. Squeeze lime juice over the top and it makes a great salad topper! If you don't want the crunchy bite, you can skip browning it under the broiler. Have it in wraps or tacos. Either way, it's a very flavorful meal!

COOKING TIME: 60 MINUTES — SERVES 8

2 lbs (907 g) frozen skinless pork shoulder, cut to fit in the pot

1 tsp sea salt

1 tsp freshly ground black pepper

1 tsp dry adobo seasoning

1 tbsp (7 g) ground cumin

1 tsp dried oregano

1 tsp garlic powder

½ cup (120 ml) bone broth

½ cup (120 ml) tomato sauce

6 cloves garlic, crushed

½ cup (80 g) diced onion

2 fresh jalapeño peppers, sliced

2 dried whole bay leaves

¼ cup (4 g) chopped fresh cilantro, divided

3 limes, 2 juiced and 1 sliced

Take the pork out of the freezer and wash it with cold water. Pat the pork dry and rub the sides with sea salt, black pepper, adobo seasoning, cumin, oregano and garlic powder. Set aside.

Add the pork shoulder, broth, tomato sauce, garlic, onion, jalapeño peppers, bay leaves and 2 tablespoons (2 g) of cilantro to the inner pot. Close the lid tightly and move the steam release handle to "Sealing." Turn on the Instant Pot by pressing the "Pressure Cooker/Manual" button and set the timer for 45 minutes on HIGH pressure.

Meanwhile, turn the oven to "Broil." Place a rack in the middle of the oven.

When the timer ends, press "Cancel" and allow the Instant Pot to cool down naturally until the float valve drops down. Open the lid carefully.

Remove the pork and pull the meat apart with a fork. Place the shredded pork on a sheet pan and place it on the rack in the oven. Bake for 10 to 15 minutes or until the top of the pork is browned.

When ready to serve, squeeze lime juice over the pork. Garnish with the remaining cilantro and lime slices, and serve immediately.

NOTE: *If you prefer soft carnitas, skip the browning in the oven. Garnish with cilantro and lime juice before serving.*

Honey BBQ Baby Back Ribs with Sweet Potato Fries

I know I have said this before about other recipes in this cookbook, but this is by far the BEST recipe to make in the Instant Pot. Hands down. I'm totally serious. And my honey BBQ sauce is also the best BBQ sauce east of the Mississippi. I'm serious about that too. And what's even better than "best"? This recipe can be made with frozen ribs and the sauce is Paleo. My work is done. You're welcome.

COOKING TIME: 30 MINUTES — SERVES 4

4 half racks of frozen pork baby back ribs

½ cup (120 ml) Honey BBQ Sauce (page 87)

1 cup (240 ml) apple cider vinegar

1 cup (240 ml) apple juice

2 (2-inch [5-cm]) pieces of fresh ginger, sliced

1 medium onion, roughly sliced

4 cloves garlic, crushed

4 sweet potatoes, sliced into ¼-inch (6-mm)-thick steak fry–shape slices

1 tbsp (15 ml) extra virgin olive oil (EVOO)

1 tsp Old Bay Seasoning

Put the frozen ribs on the cutting board and brush some of the BBQ sauce on both sides.

Place the ribs around the inner pot, with the bony ends standing up. Add apple cider vinegar, apple juice, ginger, onion and garlic to the inner pot. Close the lid tightly and move the steam release handle to "Sealing." Press the "Pressure Cooker/Manual" button and set the timer for 20 minutes (a bit chewy) or 30 minutes (fall-off-the-bone).

Meanwhile, preheat the oven to 450°F (230°C, or gas mark 8). Line a sheet pan with parchment paper. Toss the sweet potato fries in EVOO in a large mixing bowl. Sprinkle with Old Bay Seasoning and spread them on the prepared sheet pan in a single layer. Bake the fries for 30 minutes or until they are browned. Turn them over midway to bake evenly. When the fries are done, take the sheet pan out and place the fries on a wire rack to cool until serving.

When the timer ends, press "Cancel" and allow the Instant Pot to cool down naturally for 5 minutes.

Meanwhile, turn the oven to "Broil."

(continued)

Honey BBQ Baby Back Ribs with Sweet Potato Fries (continued)

After 5 minutes, carefully turn the steam release handle on the Instant Pot to the "Venting" position for the steam to escape and the float valve to drop down. Open the lid carefully and transfer the ribs to a sheet pan. Baste the ribs with the Honey BBQ Sauce. Place the sheet pan in the oven and broil each side for 1 to 2 minutes or until browned. You can also brown them on the outdoor BBQ grill. Watch the ribs carefully because the sugar in the sauce can burn very easily. Brush with more sauce, if needed. Serve with the sweet potato fries and extra BBQ sauce on the side.

NOTE: *I freeze a half rack of baby back ribs in ziplock freezer bags so they will fit inside the inner pot. You should be able to fit 2 full racks in the 6-quart (6-L) Instant Pot and 3 full racks in the 8-quart (8-L).*

Honey BBQ Sauce

COOKING TIME: 10 MINUTES — MAKES: 2 CUPS (480 ML)

¼ cup (60 ml) blackstrap unsulphured molasses

¼ cup (60 ml) Paleo Worcestershire sauce

¼ cup (60 ml) Dijon mustard

½ cup (120 ml) ketchup

¼ cup (66 g) tomato paste

¼ cup (60 ml) honey

¼ cup (60 ml) apple cider vinegar

1 large clove garlic, pressed

½ small onion

1 tsp sea salt

1 tsp freshly ground black pepper

Blend the molasses, Worcestershire sauce, Dijon mustard, ketchup, tomato paste, honey, vinegar, garlic, onion, sea salt and black pepper in a blender.

Transfer the sauce to a small sauce pot, and simmer on the stove top for 10 minutes until the sauce thickens.

Store in an airtight container in the refrigerator for up to 1 month.

Lazy Day Pulled Pork with Paleo Coleslaw

There are lazy days when I don't want to get my hands and face all messy with BBQ sauce—but I still want some BBQ meat on a bun or on a platter with veggies. Don't you have days like that? I knew you'd agree. That's why I love this Lazy Day Pulled Pork. It's so easy to make that you don't even have to defrost the pork! How simple is that? If you don't have gluten-free buns, use any green leaves to wrap the pork. Easy peasy. Lazy daisy.

COOKING TIME: 80 MINUTES — SERVES 4 TO 6

PULLED PORK

1 tbsp (15 ml) extra virgin olive oil (EVOO)

2 lbs (907 g) frozen pork butt or shoulder

1 large onion, diced

2 cloves garlic, roughly diced

1 tbsp (15 ml) apple cider vinegar

1½ cups (360 ml) Honey BBQ Sauce (page 87), divided

1 cup (240 ml) unsalted chicken broth

1 tsp dried thyme

PALEO COLESLAW

2 cups (140 g) thinly sliced green cabbage

1 cup (70 g) thinly sliced purple cabbage

½ cup (55 g) grated carrot

1 tsp sea salt, or more to taste

1½ cups (360 ml) good-quality mayonnaise

1 tsp Dijon mustard

1 tbsp (15 ml) raw honey

¼ cup (60 ml) apple cider vinegar

1 tsp celery seeds

½ tsp freshly ground black pepper

1 tbsp (4 g) chopped fresh parsley

Turn on the Instant Pot by pressing "Sauté" and set to "More." Insert the inner pot and add the EVOO and wait until the oil is hot. Add the pork and brown all sides for 3 minutes total. Even though the pork is frozen, do the best you can to brown all sides. Add the onion and garlic, and sauté for 2 to 3 minutes or until the onion is translucent.

Add the vinegar, 1 cup (240 ml) of BBQ sauce, broth and thyme to the inner pot and stir.

Close the lid tightly and move the steam release handle to "Sealing." Press "Cancel," then the "Pressure Cooker/Manual" button and set the timer for 75 minutes on HIGH pressure.

When the timer ends, allow the Instant Pot to cool down naturally until the float valve drops down. This may take between 20 to 30 minutes. Press "Cancel" and open the lid. Shred the pork using two forks and mix the meat with the liquid.

Make the coleslaw by putting the cabbages and grated carrot in a large mixing bowl. Sprinkle the cabbage with 1 teaspoon sea salt, mix well, cover the bowl and set aside for about 30 minutes. Meanwhile, in a small bowl, mix the mayonnaise, mustard, honey, apple cider vinegar, celery seeds and black pepper.

To take the moisture out of the cabbage, put the sliced cabbage in your hands and squeeze the water out. Place the cabbage in another large bowl, add the mayo mixture and mix well. Add more salt to taste.

Serve the pork immediately with the coleslaw and with extra BBQ sauce and parsley on top.

Low-Carb Memphis-Style BBQ Ribs

If your family loves BBQ ribs as much as mine does, you'll want to freeze the ribs in the shape and size of the Instant Pot because at a moment's notice, you might need to make this, just like I have. Even though I can always buy fresh ribs easily, I always have "spare" half racks of ribs in the freezer, just in case. (See what I did there?) Oh, and make a huge batch of the dry rub to use when the emergency arises. Omit the cayenne pepper if you don't want it to be spicy. This is best served with coleslaw to balance the heat.

COOKING TIME: 30 MINUTES — SERVES 6

DRY BBQ RUB

2 tbsp (16 g) chili powder

½ cup dry sweetener of your choice, like coconut sugar

¼ cup (72 g) sea salt

1 tbsp (6 g) freshly ground black pepper

2 tbsp (22 g) dry mustard

2 tbsp (14 g) ground cumin

1 tbsp (8 g) garlic powder

1 tbsp (7 g) onion powder

1 tbsp (7 g) sweet paprika

1 tsp cayenne pepper

1 tsp dried oregano

1 tsp celery seeds

2 tsp (4 g) ground turmeric

RIBS

4 frozen half racks of pork baby back ribs

1 cup (240 ml) water

½ cup (120 ml) apple cider vinegar

1 (2-inch [5-cm]) piece of fresh ginger, sliced in half vertically

Make the dry rub by mixing the chili powder, sweetener, sea salt, black pepper, dry mustard, cumin, garlic powder, onion powder, paprika, cayenne pepper, oregano, celery seeds and turmeric in a small mixing bowl. Set aside. You can store the extra rub at room temperature for 1 month.

Put the frozen ribs on the cutting board. Sprinkle about ½ cup (120 g) of the BBQ rub on each side. Place the ribs around the inner pot, bony ends standing up. You should be able to fit 2 full racks if you froze them to fit inside the pot. Add water, apple cider vinegar and ginger to the inner pot. Close the lid tightly and move the steam release handle to "Sealing." Press the "Pressure Cooker/Manual" button and set the timer for 20 minutes (a bit chewy) or 30 minutes (fall-off-the-bone).

When the timer ends, press "Cancel" and allow the Instant Pot to cool down and wait for 5 minutes. Meanwhile, turn the oven to "Broil."

After 5 minutes, carefully turn the steam release handle to the "Venting" position for the steam to escape and the float valve to drop down. Open the lid carefully and transfer the ribs to a sheet pan. Sprinkle and rub the remaining dry BBQ rub all over the ribs.

Place the sheet pan in the oven and broil each side for 4 to 5 minutes or until browned. Or you can brown them on the outdoor BBQ grill. Serve with coleslaw to balance the heat.

NOTE: *I freeze half racks of baby back ribs in ziplock freezer bags so they can fit inside the inner pot. You should be able to fit 2 full racks or 4 half racks in the 6-quart (6-L) Instant Pot. You should be able to fit 3 full racks or 5 to 6 half racks in the 8-quart (8-L) Instant Pot.*

Quick Pork Fried Rice from Scratch

Fried rice is a perfect recipe to use up leftover rice, but did you know the best fried rice is made with frozen cooked rice? That's the secret no one tells you, but I got you covered. If you can't tolerate rice, you can use cauli rice for this recipe and use 1 minute on HIGH pressure.

COOKING TIME: 12 MINUTES — SERVES 4

1 lb (454 g) frozen ground pork

½ cup (120 ml) water

1 tsp grated fresh ginger

2 tbsp (30 ml) avocado oil, divided

2 large eggs, beaten

½ cup (80 g) diced onion

1 clove garlic, minced

¼ cup (32 g) diced carrots

2 tsp (12 g) sea salt, or to taste

1 tsp ground white pepper

1 tbsp (13 g) ghee

2 cups (372 g) frozen rice or frozen cauli rice

2 cups (480 ml) unsalted chicken broth (for rice), or ½ cup (120 ml) broth (for frozen cauli rice)

1 tbsp (15 ml) toasted sesame oil

1 tbsp (9 g) sesame seeds

1 tsp black sesame seeds

¼ cup (4 g) fresh cilantro stems and leaves, divided

2 scallions, chopped and divided

Add the pork, water and ginger to the inner pot. Close the lid tightly and move the steam release handle to "Sealing." Turn on the Instant Pot by pressing the "Pressure Cooker/Manual" button and set the timer for 6 minutes on HIGH pressure.

When the timer ends, carefully turn the steam release handle to "Venting," press "Cancel" and allow the Instant Pot to depressurize quickly until the float valve drops down. Open the lid carefully. Using tongs, transfer the meat to a cutting board and cut in small pieces with a knife. Set aside.

Press "Sauté" and set to "More." Insert the inner pot and wait until the panel says "Hot." Add 1 tablespoon (15 ml) of avocado oil to the inner pot. When the oil is hot, add the beaten eggs and scramble. When the eggs are done, transfer to a small bowl and set aside.

Add the remaining avocado oil to the inner pot. When the oil is hot, add the onion, garlic and carrots. Sauté for 1 minute. Add the sea salt, white pepper, ghee and rice. Stir well for 2 minutes or until the rice is broken up and incorporated. Add the broth and scrape the bottom so the rice doesn't stick to the bottom of the pot. Add the reserved pork and stir.

Press "Cancel." Close the lid tightly and move the steam release handle to "Sealing." Press the "Pressure Cooker/Manual" button and set the timer for 3 minutes on HIGH pressure.

When the timer ends, carefully turn the steam release handle to "Venting," press "Cancel" and allow the Instant Pot to depressurize quickly until the float valve drops down. Open the lid carefully and mix well.

Add the scrambled eggs, sesame oil, sesame seeds, cilantro (reserve 1 tablespoon [1 g] for garnish) and half of the scallions. Mix while scraping the bottom of the inner pot if there is any food stuck. Transfer the fried rice to bowls, garnish with the remaining scallions and cilantro, and serve immediately.

Fins and Shells

I love cooking seafood in the Instant Pot. It only takes a few minutes and when I open the lid the ocean breeze wafts in the air. Seafood is so simple to make in the Instant Pot, and frozen seafood doesn't require that much more time than fresh seafood. Have a variety of frozen seafood on hand so when you need a quick meal, you can throw the ingredients in, press a button and set the table while dinner cooks.

Poached Atlantic Cod Antiboise (page 99) sounds very fancy, but it takes so little effort to create huge flavor. Frozen cod cooks very well, unlike other white fish. When wild cod is on sale at your fishmonger, stock up and freeze it. The Low Country Shrimp Boil (page 107) and New England Clam Bake (page 122) take a few varieties of shellfish, but they turn out so good that you wish you had a bigger Instant Pot. But my favorite recipe in this chapter is the Sweet Potato Lobster Roll (page 116). It's so simple and so quick to make that I always wish I cooked more.

Asian-Style Salmon with Ginger and Scallions

When I got married, my husband knew two recipes. One was fettuccine Alfredo out of a package that he added shrimp and broccoli to. The second one was this recipe from his mother. I was impressed he even knew these two recipes, but I was especially impressed he knew how to cook salmon perfectly. It helped that he's from the Pacific Northwest and his mother is a great cook. While he used a microwave (I know, right?) to make this recipe, I think the Instant Pot makes it even more perfect. I think my mother-in-law would be proud I'm putting her recipe in a cookbook—without using a microwave.

COOKING TIME: 6 MINUTES — SERVES 4

4 (6-oz [170-g]) frozen salmon fillets

1 cup (240 ml) water

½ cup (120 ml) tamari or ¾ cup (180 ml) coconut aminos

1 tbsp (15 ml) mirin or good-quality dry white wine

¼ cup (12 g) sliced scallion (½-inch [2-cm] pieces), divided

1 (2-inch [5-cm]) piece of fresh ginger, cut in matchsticks

1 tsp regular toasted sesame seeds

1 tsp black sesame seeds

1 tsp freshly ground black pepper

Place the salmon pieces in a glass or stainless-steel shallow plate and cover with aluminum foil. Add the water to the inner pot, place the trivet inside and the plate of covered salmon on top of the trivet. Close the lid tightly and move the steam release handle to "Sealing." Turn on the Instant Pot by pressing the "Pressure Cooker/Manual" button and set the timer for 3 minutes on HIGH pressure.

When the timer ends, press "Cancel" and allow the Instant Pot to cool down naturally until the float valve drops down. Open the lid carefully.

Uncover the plate. Try to separate the salmon pieces. Spoon the tamari and mirin over the salmon. Sprinkle the scallion (reserve 1 tablespoon [3 g] for garnish) and ginger on top. Close the lid tightly, move the steam release handle to "Sealing." Press the "Pressure Cooker/Manual" button and set the timer for 3 minutes on HIGH pressure.

When the timer ends, press "Cancel" and allow the Instant Pot to cool down naturally until the float valve drops down. Open the lid carefully.

Transfer the salmon to serving plates. Sprinkle with the sesame seeds, remaining scallions and black pepper before serving.

Poached Atlantic Cod Antiboise

Wild caught cod is our favorite white fish. It's meaty and yet tender. The mild flavor is easily adaptable, and depending on how you season it or sauce it, cod will surprise you. It's like a blank canvas for your culinary prowess. Antiboise is an umami-filled diced tomato topping with briny capers and basil. It's a light but flavorful sauce to put on top of cod without overpowering the fish. No wonder this is my daughter's favorite recipe to make for us, when she's in the mood, if I buy the groceries. Go have kids, they say.

COOKING TIME: 5 MINUTES — SERVES 4

ANTIBOISE

¼ cup (40 g) finely minced shallot

2 cloves garlic, pressed or finely minced

2 tomatoes, finely diced

1 tbsp (12 g) non-pareil capers, drained

⅓ cup (8 g) basil, thinly chiffonade

½ cup (90 g) finely chopped Kalamata olives

Zest of 1 lemon

Sea salt and freshly ground black pepper to taste

COD

¼ cup (60 ml) water

2 tbsp (30 ml) extra virgin olive oil (EVOO), divided

4 (4-oz [113-g]) frozen cod fillets (The thickest part should be no more than 1 inch [2.5 cm])

1 tsp garlic powder

½ tsp sea salt

½ tsp freshly ground black pepper

¼ cup (40 g) finely minced shallot

1 clove garlic, finely minced or pressed

½ lb (226 g) spinach (frozen or fresh)

1 tbsp (3 g) chopped fresh basil

Combine the shallot, garlic, tomatoes, capers, basil, olives and lemon zest. Add sea salt and black pepper, to taste. Refrigerate until needed. Antiboise can be made days in advance and stored in an airtight container and refrigerated for 7 to 10 days.

Insert the inner pot and add the water and 1 tablespoon (15 ml) of EVOO. Add the cod fillets, sprinkle garlic powder, sea salt and black pepper on top of the fillets. Close the lid tightly and move the steam release handle to "Sealing." Turn on the Instant Pot by pressing the "Pressure Cooker/Manual" button. Set the timer for 3 minutes on HIGH pressure.

When the timer ends, carefully turn the steam release handle to the "Venting" position for the steam to escape and the float valve to drop down. Press "Cancel," and open the lid carefully.

Carefully transfer the cod fillets and the liquid to a platter. Wipe down the inner pot and put it back in the Instant Pot.

Press "Sauté," and set to "More" until the panel says "Hot." Add the remaining EVOO to the inner pot. When the oil is hot, add the shallot and garlic and sauté for 1 minute. Add the spinach, stir and push it to one side to make room for the cod fillets. Place the cod fillets in the inner pot next to the spinach and cover the lid loosely for 1 minute.

Take out the antiboise from the refrigerator. Carefully transfer the spinach onto 4 plates. Place the cod fillets on top and spoon antiboise on top. Garnish with basil before serving.

Easy Peasy Seafood Paella

One of my best friends loves paella. But she always thought it was too much trouble to make at home—until I showed her how to make it in the Instant Pot. Then she suggested I teach her how to use frozen ingredients. What's that saying? "You give an inch, they take a mile?" Well, she's one of my best friends—so, what am I to do? I created this recipe for her.

COOKING TIMES: 11 MINUTES — SERVES 6

¼ cup (60 ml) extra virgin olive oil (EVOO)

1 medium onion, diced

6 cloves garlic, minced

1 cup (150 g) diced red bell pepper

1 cup (150 g) diced green bell pepper

½ lb (226 g) chorizo sausages, cut into 1-inch (2.5-cm) pieces

1 tbsp (12 g) non-pareil capers, drained

½ cup (90 g) diced tomatoes

10 oz (283 g) green beans, chopped

1 tsp sweet paprika

1 cup (240 ml) fish stock or chicken broth

¼ tsp saffron threads

½ tsp ground turmeric

¼ cup (4 g) chopped fresh cilantro stems and leaves, divided

⅓ cup (80 ml) good-quality dry white wine

1 tsp freshly ground black pepper

2 cups (400 g) raw rice or frozen cauli rice

4 individually frozen boneless, skinless chicken thighs

1 lb (454 g) frozen seafood mix

1 lb (454 g) large frozen shrimp with shells

Turn on the Instant Pot by pressing "Sauté" and set to "More." Insert the inner pot and wait until the panel says "Hot." Heat the EVOO and sauté the onion, garlic and bell peppers for 1 minute.

Add the chorizo sausages and sauté for 2 minutes or until the surface is no longer pink. Add the capers, tomatoes, green beans, paprika, stock, saffron, turmeric, 3 tablespoons (3 g) of cilantro, white wine and black pepper. Stir to combine. Add the rice and spread across. Place the chicken thighs on top of the rice. Do not mix.

Close the lid tightly and move the steam release handle to "Sealing."

Press "Cancel," then the "Pressure Cooker/Manual" button and set the timer for 6 minutes on HIGH pressure.

When the timer ends, carefully turn the steam release handle to "Venting," press "Cancel" and allow the Instant Pot to depressurize quickly until the float valve drops down. Open the lid carefully.

Carefully stir and mix the rice and the meat while scraping the bottom of the pot to ensure nothing is sticking to the bottom. Add the frozen seafood and shrimp on top.

Close the lid tightly and move the steam release handle to "Sealing." Press the "Pressure Cooker/Manual" button and set the timer for 2 minutes on HIGH pressure.

When the timer ends, carefully turn the steam release handle to "Venting," press "Cancel" and allow the Instant Pot to depressurize quickly until the float valve drops down. Open the lid carefully.

Spoon the paella into 6 bowls, garnish with the remaining cilantro and serve immediately.

Instant Shrimp Scampi with Capers

When I'm in a hurry to put dinner on the table but have no idea what to cook, I always reach for shrimp. Whether the shrimp is frozen or fresh, it always makes a great-tasting meal quickly. Shrimp scampi made in the Instant Pot with garlic, white wine and lemon will make anyone think you spent more time in the kitchen than you did. You can serve it over gluten-free pasta, rice or zoodles and everyone will ask for seconds. Keep a bag of frozen wild caught shrimp in the freezer and your last-minute dinner problem will be solved in no time!

COOKING TIME: 6 MINUTES — SERVES 4

1 lb (454 g) frozen extra jumbo shrimp with shells (16/20 count)

2 tbsp (26 g) ghee

2 tbsp (30 ml) extra virgin olive oil (EVOO), divided

8 cloves garlic, thinly sliced

1 cup (240 ml) good-quality dry white wine

¼ cup (60 ml) fresh lemon juice

½ tsp sea salt

½ tsp freshly ground black pepper

2 tbsp (16 g) non-pareil capers, drained

1 tsp crushed red pepper flakes (optional)

1 tbsp (4 g) chopped fresh parsley

Take out the frozen shrimp, rinse under cold water and set aside.

Turn on the Instant Pot by pressing "Sauté" and set to "More." Insert the inner pot and wait until the panel says "Hot." Add the ghee and 1 tablespoon (15 ml) of EVOO. Stir until the ghee melts. Add the garlic and sauté for 1 minute or until the garlic becomes soft. Add the frozen shrimp to the inner pot and sauté. Add the white wine and mix together.

Close the lid tightly and move the steam release handle to "Sealing." Press "Cancel," then the "Pressure Cooker/Manual" button and set the timer for 5 minutes on HIGH pressure.

When the timer ends, press "Cancel" and allow the Instant Pot to cool down naturally until the float valve drops down. Open the lid carefully.

Add the remaining EVOO, lemon juice, sea salt, black pepper, capers and crushed red pepper (if using). Stir. Transfer the shrimp and sauce to serving plates, and garnish with parsley before serving.

NOTE: *I always recommend using wild shrimp whenever possible. If you use smaller shrimp, cook 1 minute less per size count.*

Mussels in White Wine Garlic Brodo

Mussels are among the "cleanest" farmed seafood. While they filter thousands of gallons of water, they convert plankton into nutritious meaty flesh that provide a high nutritional profile. And even though they are farmed, they don't harm the marine ecosystem and are clean for human consumption. They are rich in fatty acids, EPA (eicosapentaenoic acid) and DHA (docosahexaenoic acid). Not only that, mussels are rich in vitamins and minerals, such as zinc, iron and folic acid. This easy recipe is a great appetizer to make and if you use frozen mussels, you don't even have to wash them thoroughly because they are already cleaned and debearded. Make sure to sop up the white wine garlic brodo with gluten-free bread!

COOKING TIME: 5 MINUTES — SERVES 4

3 tbsp (39 g) ghee

½ cup (80 g) finely diced shallot

2 cloves garlic, minced

Pinch of saffron threads

1 dried whole bay leaf

½ cup (120 ml) good-quality dry white wine

½ cup (120 ml) seafood stock

¼ cup (15 g) chopped fresh parsley, divided

2 lbs (907 g) frozen whole mussels

¼ cup (60 ml) fresh lemon juice

Turn on the Instant Pot by pressing "Sauté" and set to "More." Insert the inner pot and wait until the panel says "Hot."

Add the ghee in the inner pot. When the ghee is hot, add the shallot and garlic and sauté for 1 minute or until the shallot is soft. Add the saffron threads and bay leaf. Stir, then add the white wine and deglaze the bottom if needed. Add the stock and parsley (reserve 1 tablespoon [4 g] for garnish). Stir and then add the frozen mussels.

Press "Cancel." Close the lid tightly and move the steam release handle to "Sealing." Press the "Pressure Cooker/Manual" button and set the timer for 4 minutes on HIGH pressure.

When the timer ends, carefully turn the steam release handle to "Venting," press "Cancel," and allow the Instant Pot to depressurize quickly until the float valve drops down. Open the lid carefully.

Remove the bay leaf. Spoon the mussels into bowls and drizzle with lemon juice. Garnish with the remaining parsley and serve immediately.

Low Country Shrimp Boil

The best way to eat a shrimp boil is to spread everything out on a newspaper on a table. Don't worry about getting messy; just get into the potatoes, sausages and shrimp—and enjoy every spicy bite. Wear a bib if you have to, but don't be bothered by the mess. Just enjoy the spicy goodness with your sleeves rolled up.

COOKING TIME: 6 MINUTES — SERVES 6

CAJUN SEASONING

2 tsp (12 g) sea salt

2 tsp (1 g) onion powder

1 tbsp (8 g) garlic powder

2 tsp (5 g) smoked paprika

2 tsp (4 g) cayenne pepper

1 tsp freshly ground black pepper

2 tsp (2 g) dried oregano

2 tsp (1 g) dried thyme

SHRIMP

1 cup (240 ml) gluten-free beer

½ cup (120 ml) water

1 lb (454 g) small red and white potatoes or yuca, cut into 2-inch (5-cm) pieces

2 lbs (907 g) fresh or frozen smoked kielbasa or chorizo sausages, cut into 2-inch (5-cm) pieces

3 tbsp (21 g) Cajun seasoning, divided

2 tbsp (16 g) Old Bay Seasoning, divided

2 medium Vidalia onions, quartered

3 carrots, cut into 2-inch (5-cm) pieces

2 lbs (907 g) extra jumbo frozen shrimp with shells (16/20)

3 ribs celery, cut into 2-inch (5-cm) pieces

¼ cup (60 ml) melted ghee

Combine the sea salt, onion powder, garlic powder, paprika, cayenne pepper, black pepper, oregano and thyme in a bowl. You can store the extra rub in an airtight container at room temperature for up to 1 month.

Add the beer, water, potatoes and kielbasa to the inner pot. Sprinkle 1 tablespoon (7 g) of the Cajun seasoning and 1 tablespoon (8 g) of Old Bay Seasoning over the potatoes and sausages. Close the lid tightly and move the steam release handle to "Sealing." Turn on the Instant Pot by pressing the "Pressure Cooker/Manual" button and set the timer for 4 minutes on HIGH pressure.

When the timer ends, carefully turn the steam release handle to "Venting," press "Cancel" and allow the Instant Pot to depressurize quickly until the float valve drops down. Open the lid carefully. Add the onions, carrots, shrimp and celery on top. Sprinkle ½ tablespoon (about 4 g) of Cajun seasoning and ½ tablespoon (4 g) of Old Bay Seasoning on top. Close the lid tightly and move the steam release handle to "Sealing." Press the "Pressure Cooker/Manual" button and set the timer for 2 minutes on HIGH pressure.

Meanwhile, mix the remaining Cajun seasoning and Old Bay Seasoning with the melted ghee.

When the timer ends, carefully turn the steam release handle to "Venting," press "Cancel" and allow the Instant Pot to depressurize quickly until the float valve drops down. Open the lid carefully.

Transfer everything to a large platter big enough to hold everything. Drizzle the seasoned ghee on top before serving.

NOTE: *If you'd like, you can make a seafood boil by adding other seafood. Just be sure that the top layer does not go higher than the "Max" line in the inner pot.*

Octopus Salad with Fennel

Octopus usually takes a long time to cook to be tender, but it's so quick in the Instant Pot, even when it's frozen. I admit I usually buy them fresh, but when I see them on sale, I freeze them and can still make a tender and tasty recipe like this without thawing it. Another benefit to buying frozen octopus is not having to clean it since it's already cleaned before it's flash frozen! You can serve this salad warm or cold. It's simple and refreshing!

COOKING TIME: 5 MINUTES — SERVES 4

REFRIGERATOR PICKLED RED ONIONS

½ cup (120 ml) lime juice

1 lb (454 g) red onion, thinly sliced or diced

1½ cups (360 ml) extra virgin olive oil (EVOO)

1 cup (240 ml) red wine vinegar

2 tsp (4 g) dried Italian seasoning

1 tbsp (2 g) dried cilantro

OCTOPUS SALAD

¼ cup (60 ml) water

2 lbs (907 g) frozen whole octopus with tentacles

¼ cup (4 g) fresh cilantro, divided

1 cup (150 g) diced red bell pepper, divided

3 cloves garlic, minced

1 fennel frond, chopped

1 cup (101 g) thinly sliced celery

½ fennel bulb, sliced

1 tsp sea salt

½ cup (120 ml) good-quality dry white wine

½ cup (120 ml) lime juice, divided

½ cup (32 g) crushed red pepper flakes

For the refrigerator pickled red onions, combine the lime juice, red onion, EVOO, vinegar, Italian seasoning and cilantro in an airtight glass container. You can refrigerate the pickled onions for up to 1 month.

Add water and frozen octopus in the inner pot. Close the lid tightly and move the steam release handle to "Sealing." Turn on the Instant Pot by pressing the "Pressure Cooker/Manual" button and set the timer for 3 minutes on HIGH pressure.

When the timer ends, carefully turn the steam release handle to "Venting," press "Cancel" and allow the Instant Pot to depressurize quickly until the float valve drops down. Open the lid carefully.

Using tongs, transfer the octopus to a cutting board and cut the rings in ½-inch (1-cm) pieces. Put the octopus pieces back in the inner pot. Add the cilantro (reserve 1 tablespoon [1 g] for garnish), ½ cup (75 g) of bell pepper, garlic, fennel frond, celery, fennel bulb, sea salt, wine and ¼ cup (60 ml) of lime juice in the inner pot. Close the lid tightly and move the steam release handle to "Sealing." Press the "Pressure Cooker/Manual" button and set the timer for 2 minute on HIGH pressure.

Meanwhile, in a small bowl, combine the pickled red onions, remaining lime juice and crushed red pepper.

When the timer ends, carefully turn the steam release handle to "Venting," press "Cancel" and allow the Instant Pot to depressurize quickly until the float valve drops down. Open the lid carefully.

Add ½ cup (120 ml) of the pickled onion mixture to the octopus and mix. Spoon the octopus salad into serving bowls, and garnish with the remaining bell pepper and cilantro. Serve warm or cold.

Finger Lickin' Cajun Shrimp

If you love shrimp cocktail and Cajun flavors, you will love this recipe. In fact, you will be so addicted to these finger lickin' shrimp that you may need to make a double batch. After trying this amazing version, you won't go back to eating bland shrimp cocktail again. You can adjust the heat by adjusting the amount of Cajun seasoning.

COOKING TIME: 3 MINUTES — SERVES 4

2 lbs (907 g) frozen jumbo shrimp with shells (16/20)

1–2 tbsp (7–15 g) Cajun Seasoning (page 107), divided

¼ cup (60 ml) apple cider vinegar

¼ cup (60 ml) water

Insert the inner pot and place the shrimp inside. Sprinkle 1 tablespoon (about 7 g) of the Cajun seasoning all over the shrimp. Add the apple cider vinegar and water in the inner pot, and stir to mix. Close the lid tightly and move the steam release handle to "Sealing." Turn on the Instant Pot by pressing the "Pressure Cooker/Manual" button and set the timer for 3 minutes on HIGH pressure.

When the timer ends, carefully turn the steam release handle to "Venting," press "Cancel," and allow the Instant Pot to depressurize quickly until the float valve drops down. Open the lid carefully.

Sprinkle with more seasoning, if needed, before serving

Easy Salmon with Lemon and Capers over Spinach

We try to have salmon as often as we can, and this recipe is always on repeat rotation because it's so flavorful without being overpowering. And it's so easy to make, even with frozen salmon. It always comes out flaky and tender. When I'm not in the mood for my mother-in-law's Asian version (page 96), this is my go-to salmon recipe.

COOKING TIME: 6 MINUTES — SERVES 4

2 lemons, 1 sliced and 1 juiced

4 (6-oz [170-g]) frozen salmon fillets

2 tsp (8 g) non-pareil capers with liquid

1 tsp sea salt

1 tsp freshly ground black pepper

1 tbsp (15 ml) good-quality dry white wine

1 tbsp (13 g) ghee

9 oz (255 g) fresh baby spinach

1 tbsp (3 g) finely chopped fresh chives

Place the lemon slices on top of the frozen salmon and put them in a pan that fits inside the inner pot. Cover the pan loosely with aluminum foil. Put 1 cup (240 ml) of water in the inner pot. Place the trivet inside and put the covered pan on top of the trivet.

Close the lid tightly and move the steam release handle to "Sealing." Turn on the Instant Pot by pressing the "Pressure Cooker/Manual" button and set the timer for 3 minutes on HIGH pressure.

Meanwhile, in a small bowl, add the juice from 1 lemon, capers with liquid, sea salt, black pepper and white wine. Stir to combine and set aside.

When the timer ends, press "Cancel" and allow the Instant Pot to cool down naturally to depressurize until the float valve drops down. Open the lid carefully.

Remove the cover from the pan and spoon the caper mixture on top of the salmon. Close the lid tightly and move the steam release handle to "Sealing." Turn on the Instant Pot by pressing the "Pressure Cooker/Manual" button and set the timer for 3 minutes on HIGH pressure.

When the timer ends, press "Cancel" and allow the Instant Pot to cool down naturally until the float valve drops down. Open the lid carefully and take out the pan and the trivet.

Drain the water from the inner pot. Press "Sauté" and set to "More." Insert the inner pot and wait until the panel says "Hot." Add the ghee and when it's hot, add the spinach and sauté until the spinach wilts. Transfer the spinach to 4 plates. Place the salmon on top of the spinach, and garnish with chives before serving.

Louisiana Seafood Gumbo

I admit it, I'm not a huge okra fan. But somehow it works in Louisiana gumbo recipes. The brown buttery slurry makes this rich stew a winner. This freezes well, too, so make a huge batch for that busy weeknight!

COOKING TIME: 13 MINUTES — SERVES 6

¼ cup (60 ml) extra virgin olive oil (EVOO), divided

2 frozen boneless, skinless chicken thighs

½ lb (226 g) andouille or chorizo sausages, cut into 1-inch (2.5-cm) slices

1 tsp Cajun Seasoning (page 107)

2 tbsp (17 g) cassava flour

1 cup (160 g) diced onion

1 cup (150 g) diced green or red bell peppers

½ cup (51 g) diced celery

1 tbsp (9 g) minced garlic

2 cups (480 ml) unsalted chicken broth

2 tbsp (32 g) tomato paste

½ lb (226 g) frozen okra

1 tsp cayenne pepper

1 tsp dried thyme

1 tsp fish sauce

2 small dried whole bay leaves

¼ cup (15 g) chopped fresh parsley, divided

1 lb (454 g) frozen extra-large shrimp with shells on

Turn on the Instant Pot by pressing "Sauté" and set to "More." Insert the inner pot and wait until the panel says "Hot."

Add 2 tablespoons (30 ml) of EVOO to the inner pot. When the oil is hot, add the chicken thighs and the sausages and brown them as well as you can. Add the Cajun seasoning and stir. Sauté for about 3 minutes. Transfer the meat to a plate with a slotted spoon.

Add the remaining EVOO and the cassava flour to the pot and stir for about 3 minutes until it turns brown. Add the onion, peppers, celery and garlic, and stir for about 1 minute until the vegetables become a little soft. Add the broth to deglaze the bottom of the pot. Add the tomato paste, okra, cayenne pepper, thyme, fish sauce, bay leaves and parsley (reserve 2 tablespoons [8 g] for garnish). Stir to incorporate. Stir in the chicken thighs and sausages.

Press "Cancel." Close the lid tightly and move the steam release handle to "Sealing." Press the "Pressure Cooker/Manual" button and set the timer for 6 minutes on HIGH pressure.

When the timer ends, carefully turn the steam release handle to "Venting," press "Cancel," and allow the Instant Pot to depressurize quickly until the float valve drops down. Open the lid carefully.

Stir and scrape the bottom of the pan. Add the frozen shrimp and stir to combine. Close the lid for 5 minutes or until the shrimp are pink and cooked.

Remove the bay leaves. Spoon the seafood into 6 bowls, garnish with the remaining parsley and serve immediately.

Sweet Potato Lobster Roll

It wouldn't be summer if there was no lobster roll. I love making them because they're so easy, and they're delicious with dripping clarified butter (ghee) and a side of refreshing coleslaw. My children couldn't eat bread, and I used to serve it as a salad which just wasn't quite the same. Then, I figured out that sweet potatoes make perfect rolls for this quintessential summer lunch! I think you will love it, too! And if you use frozen lobster tails, there's less mess and it's even easier!

COOKING TIME: 17 MINUTES — SERVES 4

4 (4-oz [113-g]) sweet potatoes

4 (6-oz [170-g]) frozen lobster tails

2–4 tbsp (26–52 g) ghee, divided

Sea salt, to taste

Freshly ground black pepper, to taste

¼ cup (12 g) chopped fresh chives

Paleo Coleslaw (page 88)

Wash the sweet potatoes well. Put 2 cups (480 ml) water in the inner pot and place the trivet inside. Put the sweet potatoes on the trivet. Close the lid tightly and move the steam release handle to "Sealing." Turn on the Instant Pot by pressing the "Pressure Cooker/Manual" button and set the timer for 12 minutes on HIGH pressure.

Meanwhile, take out the lobster tails from the freezer, run them under cold water. Set aside.

When the timer ends, carefully turn the steam release handle to "Venting," press "Cancel" and allow the Instant Pot to depressurize quickly until the float valve drops down. Open the lid carefully.

Take out the sweet potatoes and set aside. Put the lobster tails on the trivet—stack them if needed—close the lid tightly and move the steam release handle to "Sealing." Press the "Pressure Cooker/Manual" button and set the timer for 5 minutes on HIGH pressure.

When the timer ends, carefully turn the steam release handle to "Venting," press "Cancel" and allow the Instant Pot to depressurize quickly until the float valve drops down. Open the lid carefully.

(continued)

Sweet Potato Lobster Roll (continued)

Using tongs, take out the lobster tails and place them on a cutting board. Take the meat out of the lobster shells and cut them into 1-inch (2.5-cm) pieces and set aside.

Make a slit on the tops of the sweet potatoes.

Press "Sauté" and add 2 tablespoons (26 g) of ghee to the inner pot. Add the lobster tail pieces and quickly sauté. Add up to 2 tablespoons (26 g) more of ghee, if needed, to keep the lobster meat from sticking to the pot. Sprinkle sea salt and freshly ground black pepper, to taste.

Spoon the lobster meat onto the sweet potatoes, garnish with chives and serve immediately with a side of Paleo Coleslaw (page 88).

Shrimp with Lobster Sauce

Who loves shrimp with lobster sauce? (Raises both hands.) Seriously though, this is a dish that no one can classify correctly. It's served alone so it's not really a sauce. It's not a stew because it's a bit thin and watery. But it's never in the soup section of the menu so you can't order it as a soup. Furthermore, it doesn't even have any lobster! The dish is always confusing. One thing is for sure: It tastes great and it's easy to make in the Instant Pot. So, who's complaining?

COOKING TIME: 5 MINUTES — SERVES 4

8 oz (226 g) frozen ground pork

2 tbsp (30 ml) avocado oil

2 cloves garlic, grated or finely minced

1 tbsp (15 ml) good-quality dry white wine

2 cups (480 ml) chicken stock

30 large frozen shrimp, shelled and deveined

1 tsp fish sauce

1 cup (110 g) chopped string beans

1 cup (70 g) sliced fresh shiitake mushrooms

½ tsp sea salt

2 tbsp (16 g) tapioca flour

2 large eggs

2 scallions, chopped and divided

½ tsp white pepper

1 tsp sesame oil, divided

Cooked rice or cauli rice

Put 1 cup (240 ml) water in the inner pot and place the ground pork inside. Close the lid tightly and move the steam release handle to "Sealing." Turn on the Instant Pot by pressing the "Pressure Cooker/Manual" button and set the timer for 2 minutes on HIGH pressure.

When the timer ends, carefully turn the steam release handle to "Venting," press "Cancel" and allow the Instant Pot to depressurize quickly until the float valve drops down. Open the lid carefully.

Using tongs, transfer the meat to a cutting board and chop it into small ½-inch (1-cm) pieces with a knife. Set aside.

Drain the liquid from the inner pot and wipe it down. Add the avocado oil to the inner pot. Press "Sauté" and wait until the panel says "Hot." When the oil is hot, add the garlic and sauté for 1 minute or until the garlic is soft. Add the wine and deglaze the pot. Add the reserved ground pork, stock, shrimp, fish sauce, string beans, mushrooms and sea salt.

Press "Cancel." Close the lid tightly and move the steam release handle to "Sealing." Press the "Pressure Cooker/Manual" button and set the timer for 2 minutes on HIGH pressure.

(continued)

Shrimp with Lobster Sauce (continued)

Meanwhile, in a small bowl, combine the tapioca flour and 3 tablespoons (45 ml) of water to make a slurry. In another small bowl, beat 2 eggs slightly.

When the timer ends, turn the steam release handle to "Venting," press "Cancel," and allow the Instant Pot to depressurize quickly until the float valve drops down. Open the lid carefully.

Press "Sauté." Slowly pour in the slurry while stirring. When the liquid is thickened, add the scallions (reserve 1 tablespoon [3 g] for garnish), white pepper and sesame oil. Stir.

Slowly drizzle the beaten egg and stir occasionally. It may take about 2 minutes before the eggs are cooked. When they are cooked, ladle the "sauce" into 4 bowls with rice and garnish with the reserved scallions before serving.

New England Clam Bake

Summer is made for clam bakes. Or do clam bakes make the summer? But what happens when the weather doesn't cooperate? No worries. The Instant Pot is ready to report for duty to carry on the tradition, all year round, even with frozen seafood! So, make sure to freeze some clams next time you go clamming so you'll have them for this weatherproof clam bake in your kitchen!

COOKING TIME: 8 MINUTES — SERVES 4

2 tbsp (30 ml) extra virgin olive oil (EVOO), divided

4 oz (113 g) frozen or fresh chorizo, kielbasa or beef hot dog, cut into 2- to 3-inch (5- to 7.5-cm) slices

1 (12-oz [340-ml]) can gluten-free beer

1 cup (240 ml) fish or chicken stock

3 small dried whole bay leaves

1 tbsp (3 g) dried thyme

1 tbsp (3 g) dried tarragon

2 tbsp (30 ml) fish sauce

½ lb (226 g) small red and white potatoes (optional)

20 little neck clams, de-sanded, frozen or fresh

1 lb (454 g) extra-large frozen shrimp with shells

4 oz (113 g) seaweed or kombu, rehydrated

1 small onion, thickly sliced

2 ribs celery, cut in half

2 medium-sized carrots, cut in half

¼ cup (60 ml) fresh lemon juice

2 tbsp (8 g) chopped fresh parsley

Turn on the Instant Pot by pressing "Sauté" and set to "More." Insert the inner pot and wait until the panel says "Hot."

Add 1 tablespoon (15 ml) of EVOO to the inner pot. When the oil is hot, add the chorizo and sauté to brown as well as you can for 2 minutes. Add the beer and stock and deglaze the pot, if needed. Stir in the bay leaves, thyme, tarragon and fish sauce. In this order add the potatoes (if using), clams, shrimp, seaweed, onion, celery and carrots.

Press "Cancel." Close the lid tightly and move the steam release handle to "Sealing."

Press the "Pressure Cooker/Manual" button and set the timer for 6 minutes on LOW pressure.

When the timer ends, press "Cancel" and allow the Instant Pot to cool down naturally until the float valve drops down. Open the lid carefully.

Remove the bay leaves. Transfer to a large serving platter or a sheet pan. Drizzle with the lemon juice, garnish with parsley and serve immediately.

Slurping Noodles

I am so glad there are more gluten-free noodles and pasta available now. When we started Paleo, there weren't too many options. Now, we are thrilled to find rice noodles in all shapes and forms to make dishes such as Penne with Italian Sausage and Peppers (page 129), Short Ribs Ragu for Pasta (page 133), Shrimp fra Diavolo over Penne (page 137) and Baked Gluten-Free Ziti with Meat Sauce (page 138). Of course, there's our favorite, Sweet Potato Noodles with Beef (Japchae) (page 134), a dish that I grew up with. If you prefer zoodles, you'll love Quick Zoodles Bolognese (page 130).

If you can't tolerate rice noodles, you can always use zoodles or spaghetti squash for any of these recipes. Regardless of what kind of noodles you prefer, these sauces that you can make with frozen ingredients will put amazing meals on the table fast!

NOTE: *The general rule for cooking pasta in the Instant Pot is to use thick pasta, such as penne or ziti, and half the time listed on the package directions.*

One-Pot Penne with Mussels in Marinara Sauce

When I first learned you can make pasta in the Instant Pot, I didn't believe it. The trick is to undercook them slightly—especially gluten-free types that are quicker to cook—then simmer for a few minutes without the lid until al dente. You will never cook pasta on the stove top after learning how easy it is to cook in the Instant Pot. No more multiple pots and strainers to wash!

COOKING TIME: 6 MINUTES — SERVES 4

3 tbsp (45 ml) extra virgin olive oil (EVOO)

1 medium onion, chopped

3 cloves garlic, pressed

1 cup (240 ml) pasta sauce of your choice

1 tbsp (7 g) Italian seasoning

1 tsp sea salt, divided

1 tsp freshly ground black pepper

1 cup (240 ml) water

1 lb (454 g) brown rice penne or zoodles (See the Noodles Tip for instructions on using zoodles or spaghetti squash.)

2 lbs (907 g) of frozen whole mussels

1 tbsp (4 g) chopped fresh parsley

Turn on the Instant Pot by pressing "Sauté" and set to "More." Insert the inner pot and wait until the panel says "Hot."

Add the EVOO to the inner pot. When the oil is hot, add the onion and garlic. Sauté for 1 minute or until the onion is soft. Add the sauce, Italian seasoning, sea salt and black pepper. Stir, then add the water and the penne. Make sure the pasta is submerged in liquid. If not, add more water. Add the mussels on top.

Press "Cancel." Close the lid tightly and move the steam release handle to "Sealing." Press the "Pressure Cooker/Manual" button and set the timer for 5 minutes on LOW pressure.

When the timer ends, carefully turn the steam release handle to "Venting," press "Cancel," and allow the Instant Pot to depressurize quickly until the float valve drops down. Open the lid carefully. Stir to mix the pasta. If the pasta is undercooked, stir and let it simmer, uncovered, until it's cooked al dente. Garnish with parsley and serve immediately.

NOODLES TIP: *To use spaghetti squash in the recipe, cook the spaghetti squash first. Place a whole spaghetti squash on a trivet in the inner pot, pour 1 cup (240 ml) of water in the inner pot, and cook on HIGH pressure for 15 minutes. Carefully turn the steam release handle to "Venting," press "Cancel" and allow the Instant Pot to depressurize quickly until the float valve drops down. Open the lid carefully. Take out the spaghetti squash and cut around the shorter diameter. Scoop out the seeds and loosen the strands with a fork and set aside to top it with sauce.*

If using zoodles, spiralize the zucchini and quickly stir it into the inner pot with sauce before serving.

Penne with Italian Sausage and Peppers

Italian sausage and peppers on a roll is one of my husband's favorite sammies. But because Emily and Andrew can't eat bread, I always make a pasta version with gluten-free penne in the Instant Pot. And since I figured out how to use frozen sausages, it's a simple lunch on a busy weekend for us. If you don't want to use gluten-free pasta, you can always use spaghetti squash or zoodles!

COOKING TIME: 7 MINUTES — SERVES 4

3 tbsp (45 ml) extra virgin olive oil (EVOO), divided

1 lb (454 g) frozen sweet Italian sausages

1 medium onion, sliced

4 cloves garlic, minced

2 yellow or red bell peppers, sliced

1 cup (240 ml) good-quality dry red wine

1 tsp sea salt

1 tsp freshly ground black pepper

½ tsp dried oregano

1 tbsp (7 g) Italian seasoning

½ cup (30 g) chopped fresh parsley, divided

¼ cup (10 g) chopped fresh basil, divided

2 cups (360 g) diced tomatoes

1 tbsp (16 g) tomato paste

1 cup (240 ml) water

1 cup (105 g) brown rice penne (See the Noodles Tip on page 126)

Take the sausages out of the package. Rinse under cold running water and separate the links. Set aside.

Turn on the Instant Pot by pressing "Sauté" and set to "More." Insert the inner pot and wait until the panel says "Hot."

Add 1 tablespoon (15 ml) of EVOO to the inner pot. When the oil is hot, add the sausages and brown the outside as well as you can. The oil might splatter so be careful. Using tongs, transfer the sausages to a cutting board and cut into 1-inch (2.5-cm) pieces. Set aside.

Add the remaining EVOO. When the oil is hot, add the onion and garlic and sauté for 1 minute or until the onion is soft. Add the bell peppers and sauté for 1 minute. Add the wine and deglaze the pot, if needed. Add the sea salt, black pepper, oregano, Italian seasoning, parsley (reserve 1 tablespoon [4 g] for garnish), basil (reserve 1 tablespoon [3 g] for garnish), tomatoes and the tomato paste. Stir until everything is incorporated. Add the sausages and mix. Add the water and penne on top. Don't mix but make sure the pasta is submerged in liquid. If not, add more water.

Press "Cancel." Close the lid tightly and move the steam release handle to "Sealing."

Press the "Pressure Cooker/Manual" button and set the timer for 5 minutes on LOW pressure.

When the timer ends, carefully turn the steam release handle to "Venting," press "Cancel" and allow the Instant Pot to depressurize quickly until the float valve drops down. Open the lid carefully.

Stir to mix the pasta. If the pasta is undercooked, stir and let it simmer, uncovered, until it's cooked al dente. Garnish with remaining parsley and basil, and serve immediately.

Quick Zoodles Bolognese

Pasta Bolognese is a fancy term for spaghetti with meat sauce. Spaghetti can be tricky to cook in the Instant Pot, so I prefer using zoodles or spaghetti squash. For a quick meal, zoodles work better than spaghetti squash because you don't even need to cook the zoodles. Who's with me?

COOKING TIME: 6 MINUTES — SERVES 4

1 lb (454 g) frozen ground beef

2 tbsp (30 ml) extra virgin olive oil (EVOO)

1 small onion, finely chopped

4 cloves garlic, minced

½ cup (120 ml) good-quality dry red wine

2 cups (480 ml) your favorite marinara sauce

2 tbsp (32 g) tomato paste

1½ tsp (9 g) sea salt, divided

¼ cup (10 g) chopped fresh basil, divided

¼ cup (15 g) chopped fresh parsley, divided

3 zucchinis, spiralized into zoodles

Add the ground beef and 1 cup (240 ml) of water to the inner pot. Close the lid tightly and move the steam release handle to "Sealing." Turn on the Instant Pot by pressing the "Pressure Cooker/Manual" button and set the timer for 3 minutes on HIGH pressure.

When the timer ends, carefully turn the steam release handle to "Venting," press "Cancel" and allow the Instant Pot to depressurize quickly until the float valve drops down. Open the lid carefully.

Using tongs, transfer the meat to a cutting board and chop it into small pieces with a knife. Reserve the liquid in a small bowl and set aside. Wipe down the inner pot, and add the EVOO.

Press "Sauté" and set to "More." Insert the inner pot and wait until the panel says "Hot."

When the oil is hot, add the onion and garlic. Sauté for 1 minute or until the onion is soft. Add the red wine and deglaze the pot. Add the beef back to the inner pot, reserved broth, marinara sauce, tomato paste, 1 teaspoon of sea salt, basil (reserve 1 tablespoon [3 g] for garnish) and parsley (reserve 1 tablespoon [4 g] for garnish). Stir well.

Press "Cancel." Close the lid tightly and move the steam release handle to "Sealing." Press the "Pressure Cooker/Manual" button and set the timer for 3 minutes on HIGH pressure.

Meanwhile, spiralize the zucchinis, sprinkle with the remaining sea salt and set aside.

When the timer ends, press "Cancel" and allow the Instant Pot to cool down naturally until the float valve drops down. Open the lid carefully.

Stir the sauce well. With tongs, place the zoodles onto 4 shallow plates. Spoon the Bolognese sauce on top of the zoodles, garnish with the remaining basil and parsley, and serve immediately.

Short Ribs Ragu for Pasta

Short rib meat is a great choice over pasta! If you can find gluten-free egg noodles, this recipe will become your favorite pasta sauce for it. Because the meat needs to be really tender, it does require a bit longer to cook, but you can use frozen short ribs so you don't have to wait for the meat to defrost!

COOKING TIME: 60 MINUTES — SERVES 6

1 tbsp (13 g) ghee

1 small onion

5 cloves garlic, crushed

1 lb (454 g) frozen short ribs

1 cup (240 ml) good-quality dry red wine

1 tbsp (15 ml) balsamic vinegar

¼ cup (15 g) chopped fresh parsley, divided

¼ cup (6 g) loosely packed basil

1 sprig of fresh rosemary

1 sprig of fresh thyme

1 sprig of fresh tarragon

2 carrots, cut in 1-inch (2.5-cm) cuts diagonally

2 cups (480 ml) pasta sauce of your choice

2 tbsp (32 g) tomato paste

½ tsp sea salt

½ tsp freshly ground black pepper

1⅔ cups (8 oz [226 g]) white mushrooms, sliced

Turn on the Instant Pot by pressing "Sauté" and set to "More." Insert the inner pot and wait until the panel says "Hot."

Add the ghee to the inner pot. When the ghee is hot, add the onion and garlic. Sauté for 1 minute or until the onion is soft. Add the ribs and brown as well as you can. Add the red wine and balsamic vinegar to deglaze the bottom of the pot. Add the parsley (reserve 1 tablespoon [4 g] for garnish), basil, rosemary, thyme, tarragon, carrots, pasta sauce, tomato paste, sea salt, black pepper and mushrooms.

Press "Cancel." Close the lid tightly and move the steam release handle to "Sealing." Press the "Pressure Cooker/Manual" button and set the timer for 45 minutes on HIGH pressure.

When the timer ends, press "Cancel" and allow the Instant Pot to naturally cool down for 15 minutes. Then, carefully turn the steam release handle to "Venting," and allow the Instant Pot to depressurize quickly until the float valve drops down. Open the lid carefully and stir.

Take out the meat, shred it, return it to the sauce and stir. Serve hot with your favorite pasta.

NOTES: *If using the short rib ragu over zoodles, add the spiralized zucchini to the pot after the ragu is done, close the lid and let the zoodles cook for 5 minutes. Garnish with the remaining parsley and serve immediately. If using gluten-free pasta, cook the pasta separately and use the ragu as the sauce on top.*

If possible, always cut the short ribs in between the bones, and freeze individual pieces in a ziplock bag. It will be quicker to cook when needed. Run the ribs under cold running water to separate them before cooking. If you forget to cut them and you have a big chunk of ribs, cook them 15 minutes longer and shred them afterward. You might not be able to brown them well, but the meat will still be tender.

Sweet Potato Noodles with Beef (Japchae)

Japchae is a quintessential Korean noodle dish that is usually complicated but I figured out how to make everything in the Instant Pot. You don't even have to use a fancy cut of meat! You can thank me later.

COOKING TIME: 12 MINUTES — SERVES 4

6 oz (170 g) sweet potato noodles, glass noodles or japchae noodles

4 cups (960 ml) warm water, divided

2 tbsp (30 ml) avocado oil, divided

1 lb (454 g) frozen ground beef

2 tbsp (30 ml) tamari or coconut aminos, divided

2 tsp (10 ml) sesame oil, divided

1 small onion, thinly sliced

2 cloves garlic, minced

1 (1-inch [2.5-cm]) piece of fresh ginger, grated

1 small carrot, thinly julienned

1 cup (70 g) thinly sliced fresh shitake mushrooms

½ cup (75 g) thinly sliced red bell pepper

1 tbsp (15 ml) mirin or rice wine

3 cups (90 g) fresh baby spinach

1 tsp roasted sesame seeds

2 scallions, finely chopped

Sea salt and freshly ground black pepper, to taste

Take the noodles out of the package and break them into 8-inch (20-cm) sections. Put 3 cups (720 ml) of the warm water in a large bowl and soak the noodles for 2 minutes.

Turn on the Instant Pot by pressing "Sauté" and set to "More." Insert the inner pot and wait until the panel says "Hot." Add 1 tablespoon (15 ml) of avocado oil to the inner pot. When the oil is hot, carefully add the frozen beef to brown for about 1 minute on its sides. Add the remaining water and 1 tablespoon (15 ml) of tamari to the inner pot. Press "Cancel." Close the lid tightly and move the steam release handle to "Sealing." Press the "Pressure Cooker/Manual" button and set the timer for 5 minutes on HIGH pressure.

Meanwhile, strain the sweet potato noodles. The noodles will be stiff but don't worry. They will get cooked thoroughly later.

When the timer ends, carefully turn the steam release handle to "Venting," press "Cancel," and allow the Instant Pot to depressurize until the float valve drops down. Open the lid carefully. Transfer the meat to a cutting board and chop the meat into small pieces. Set aside. Strain the broth into a small bowl and set aside. Wipe down the inner pot and add the remaining avocado oil and 1 teaspoon of sesame oil. When the oil is hot, sauté the onion, garlic and ginger for 1 minute. Add the carrot, mushrooms and bell pepper. Sauté for 1 minute or until the peppers are soft. Add the remaining tamari, mirin, reserved meat and the reserved meat broth to the inner pot. Spread the sweet potato noodles on top, in a crisscross manner; do not mix or stir.

Close the lid tightly and move the steam release handle to "Sealing." Press the "Pressure Cooker/Manual" button and set the timer for 3 minutes on HIGH pressure. When the timer ends, carefully turn the steam release handle to "Venting," press "Cancel" and allow the Instant Pot to depressurize until the float valve drops down. Open the lid carefully. Add the spinach, remaining sesame oil, sesame seeds and scallions (reserve 1 tablespoon [3 g] for garnish). Mix with tongs, and sprinkle with sea salt and black pepper, to taste. Garnish with the reserved scallions and serve immediately.

Shrimp fra Diavolo over Penne

I tend to sprinkle crushed red pepper on everything and anything, so shrimp fra diavolo is one of my favorite Italian pasta dishes. The beauty of making it in the Instant Pot is that I don't have to defrost the shrimp and I can cook the pasta at the same time. No messy stove top and fewer pots and pans to wash afterward.

COOKING TIME: 7 MINUTES — SERVES 4

1 lb (454 g) frozen large shrimp, peeled and deveined

3 tbsp (45 ml) extra virgin olive oil (EVOO)

1 medium onion, sliced

3 cloves garlic, pressed or finely minced

2 cups (360 g) diced tomatoes

1 tbsp (16 g) tomato paste

1 cup (240 ml) white wine, such as chardonnay or pinot grigio

1 tbsp (7 g) Italian seasoning

1 tsp sea salt

2 tsp (2 g) crushed red pepper flakes, or more to taste

¼ cup (6 g) fresh basil, chopped

¼ cup (15 g) chopped fresh parsley, divided

1 cup (240 ml) water

1 cup (105 g) brown rice penne (See the Noodles Tip page 126)

Rinse the frozen shrimp under running cold water to remove any debris. Set aside.

Turn on the Instant Pot by pressing "Sauté" and set to "More." Insert the inner pot and wait until the panel says "Hot."

Add the EVOO to the inner pot. When the oil is hot, add the onion and garlic. Sauté for 1 minute or until the onion is soft. Add the shrimp and sauté for 1 minute. Add the tomatoes, tomato paste, wine, Italian seasoning, sea salt, crushed red pepper, basil and parsley (reserve 1 tablespoon [4 g] for garnish). Stir. Add the water and place the penne on top but do not mix. Make sure the pasta is submerged in liquid.

Press "Cancel." Close the lid tightly and move the steam release handle to "Sealing." Press the "Pressure Cooker/Manual" button and set the timer for 5 minutes on LOW pressure.

When the timer ends, carefully turn the steam release handle to "Venting," press "Cancel" and allow the Instant Pot to depressurize quickly until the float valve drops down. Open the lid carefully.

Mix the pasta and shrimp. If the pasta is cooked, ladle the pasta and shrimp into 4 bowls, garnish with the remaining parsley and serve immediately. If the pasta is undercooked, leave the lid open and press "Sauté" and simmer. Stir occasionally until it's cooked al dente. Garnish with the remaining parsley and serve immediately.

Baked Gluten-Free Ziti with Meat Sauce

I used to bring my "famous" baked ziti to potluck dinners and big gatherings. Baked ziti is such a comfort food that it's popular all year round. But who wants to turn on the oven in the middle of the summer when you can make it in the Instant Pot? All you need the oven for is to brown the top for a couple of minutes! Now that there are many gluten-free pastas available, Paleo-style baked pasta is easy and fun to make for any occasion.

COOKING TIME: 18 MINUTES — SERVES 6

2 tbsp (30 ml) extra virgin olive oil (EVOO), divided

½ lb (226 g) frozen ground beef

½ lb (226 g) frozen sweet Italian sausage

1 medium onion, diced

3 cloves garlic, minced

1 tbsp (4 g) crushed red pepper flakes

1 tsp sea salt

½ tsp freshly ground black pepper

1 tsp Italian seasoning

½ cup (120 ml) good-quality dry red wine

½ cup (20 g) chopped fresh basil, divided

1 cup (240 ml) water

2 cups (480 ml) your favorite marinara sauce

1 tbsp (16 g) tomato paste

1 cup (105 g) brown rice ziti or penne

1 cup (80 g) grated Pecorino Romano cheese (optional)

Turn on the Instant Pot by pressing "Sauté" and set to "More." Insert the inner pot and wait until the panel says "Hot."

Add 1 tablespoon (15 ml) of EVOO to the inner pot. When the oil is hot, add the ground beef and sausage and brown the outside for 2 minutes or as well as you can. The oil might splatter so be careful. Using tongs, transfer the ground beef and sausage to a cutting board and cut in small pieces with a knife. Set aside.

Add the remaining EVOO and when the oil is hot, add the onion and garlic. Sauté for 1 minute or until the onion is soft. Add the crushed red pepper, sea salt, black pepper and Italian seasoning. Stir, then add the wine and deglaze the pot, if needed. Add the beef and sausage and mix to combine. In the following order, add the basil (reserve 1 tablespoon [3 g] for garnish), water, pasta sauce and tomato paste. Lastly, add the ziti on top and don't mix. Make sure the ziti is submerged in liquid. If it's not, add more water.

Press "Cancel." Close the lid tightly and move the steam release handle to "Sealing." Press the "Pressure Cooker/Manual" button and set the timer for 5 minutes on LOW pressure.

Meanwhile, preheat the oven to 400°F (200°C, or gas mark 6).

When the timer ends, carefully turn the steam release handle to "Venting," press "Cancel" and allow the Instant Pot to depressurize quickly until the float valve drops down. Open the lid carefully.

Stir to mix the pasta. Transfer the ziti to an ovenproof 9 x 11–inch (23 x 28–cm) glass pan. Sprinkle the top with grated Pecorino Romano cheese (if using). Bake the ziti for 10 minutes or until the top is browned. Garnish with basil before serving.

Shoyu Ramen

Ramen is one of the noodle dishes that my family missed when we went on the Paleo diet. Then I figured out how to make the ramen broth and now that they can tolerate rice noodles, we are so happy to have ramen back in our lives again. If you can tolerate rice, I strongly recommend you try this ramen recipe. I make a large batch of the broth and freeze it for whenever we feel like having ramen.

COOKING TIME: 18 MINUTES — SERVES 8

SHOYU BROTH

2 dried shiitake mushrooms

1 cup (240 ml) cold water

10 oz (200 g) dried kombu

2 cups (480 ml) hot water

½ rack frozen baby back ribs

4 frozen boneless, skinless chicken thighs

3 scallions

1 (1-inch [2.5-cm]) piece of ginger, sliced

6 cloves garlic, crushed

2 tbsp (30 ml) tamari or coconut aminos

1 tbsp (15 ml) mirin

4 cups (960 ml) chicken stock

RAMEN NOODLES

6 cups (1.4 L) water

4 large eggs

1 carrot, julienned

4 oz (113 g) Napa cabbage, sliced

2 fresh shiitake mushrooms, sliced

4 servings of rice ramen noodles (See the Noodles Tip on page 126)

1 scallion, chopped

1 tsp black sesame seeds

1 tsp toasted sesame seeds

To make the broth, in a small bowl, soak the dried shiitake mushrooms in the cold water and set aside. In a medium-sized bowl, soak the kombu in the hot water and set aside. Insert the inner pot. Add the ribs, chicken thighs, scallions, ginger, garlic, tamari, mirin, stock, shiitake mushrooms and kombu (including their soaking water). Close the lid tightly and move the steam release handle to "Sealing." Turn on the Instant Pot by pressing the "Pressure Cooker/Manual" button and set the timer for 15 minutes on HIGH pressure.

When the timer ends, press "Cancel" and allow the Instant Pot to cool down naturally until the float valve drops down. Open the lid carefully.

Strain the broth, cover and set aside. Transfer the chicken thighs to a plate and set aside. Discard the rest of the ingredients.

To make the rice ramen noodles, insert the inner pot. Add 6 cups (1.4 L) water, whole eggs, carrots, Napa cabbage and mushrooms. Place the ramen noodles on top and make sure they are immersed in the liquid. Do not mix. Close the lid tightly and move the steam release handle to "Sealing." Turn on the Instant Pot by pressing the "Pressure Cooker/Manual" button and set the timer for 3 minutes on LOW pressure.

When the timer ends, carefully turn the steam release handle to "Venting," press "Cancel" and allow the Instant Pot to depressurize quickly until the float valve drops down. Open the lid carefully.

Using tongs, transfer the noodles to 4 bowls. Take out the eggs, peel them and cut them in half. Top the bowls with the reserved chicken thighs, hard boiled eggs, vegetables and scallion. Sprinkle with sesame seeds. Pour the reserved shoyu broth into the bowls and serve immediately.

Steaming Soups and Stews

Soups and stews make hearty meals, especially when you are pressed for time. They are easy to whip up and perfect for using frozen meats. Add fresh vegetables and herbs and you have a meal to satisfy even the hungriest linebacker.

There are some classic soups in this chapter, such as Chicken and Dumplings Soup (page 168), Healthy Beef and Vegetable Soup (page 147), Italian Sausage and Escarole Soup (page 151) and Mrs. Chen's Egg Drop Soup (page 171). But I've also Paleotized a Dairy-Free Zuppa Toscana (page 148) and Chicken Potpie Soup (page 144) for those times when you need your childhood favorites.

Chicken Potpie Soup

Chicken potpie is the ultimate comfort food, so how about making it into a soup? I thought you'd like that idea too, so I came up with a way to make it into a warm soothing soup for those days when life throws you a curve ball. Even if you forget to defrost the chicken, I've got you covered.

COOKING TIME: 38 MINUTES — SERVES 4

2 tbsp (26 g) ghee, divided

1 tbsp (9 g) minced garlic

½ cup (80 g) diced onion

1 lb (454 g) frozen boneless, skinless chicken thighs

1 cup (128 g) carrots, cut into ½-inch (1-cm) cubes

1 cup (128 g) celery, cut into ½-inch (1-cm) cubes

1 cup (150 g) cubed potato or yuca

¼ cup (15 g) finely chopped fresh parsley, divided

1 tsp dried basil

1 tsp dried oregano

1 tsp dried thyme

1 tsp dried tarragon

1 large dried whole bay leaf

1 tbsp (18 g) sea salt

1 tsp freshly ground black pepper

3 cups (720 ml) unsalted chicken broth

1 tbsp (8 g) tapioca flour

¼ cup (60 ml) cold water

NOTE: *You can also use arrowroot powder or cassava flour as thickeners.*

Turn on the Instant Pot by pressing "Sauté" and set to "More." Insert the inner pot and wait until the panel says "Hot."

Add 1 tablespoon (13 g) of ghee to the inner pot and stir until it's hot. Add the garlic and onion, and sauté for 1 minute. Add the chicken thighs and brown each side as well as you can, 1 minute per side. They don't have to get a deep golden color, as long as they become opaque. Add the remaining ghee, carrots, celery and potato. Sauté for 1 minute. Add the fresh parsley (reserve 1 tablespoon [4 g] for garnish) basil, oregano, thyme, tarragon, bay leaf, sea salt and black pepper. Stir well. Add the chicken broth and stir to cover all the ingredients.

Press "Cancel." Close the lid tightly and move the steam release handle to "Sealing."

Press the "Pressure Cooker/Manual" button and set the timer for 20 minutes on HIGH pressure.

Meanwhile, make a slurry by combining the tapioca flour with cold water in a small bowl and set aside.

When the timer ends, allow the Instant Pot to cool down naturally for 10 minutes. Press "Cancel," then carefully turn the steam release handle to "Venting" and let out the steam. Open the lid carefully.

Shred the chicken in the pot if you can. If it's easier, transfer the chicken thighs to a cutting board and cut them into smaller pieces. If the chicken is not fully cooked, don't worry; it will be fully cooked by the time cooking is done. Place all the chicken pieces back into the inner pot and stir in the tapioca slurry to thicken.

Click "Sauté" until it's on "Normal." Simmer for 5 minutes while stirring occasionally. Remove the bay leaf. When ready to serve, ladle the soup into 4 bowls and garnish with the remaining parsley.

Healthy Beef and Vegetable Soup

When I was in high school, I remember having a can of "beef and vegetable soup" when there was nothing to eat in the house after school. I thought it was filled with "meat and vegetables" and the aroma from the hot piping soup always made me feel "nourished." Sadly, I learned later on that the soup didn't have a lot of real meat and vegetables. It was mostly fillers and processed chemicals. So, I wanted to make my childhood memories legit by creating the soup using only real ingredients. With the Instant Pot, I love it even more because I can make it with frozen beef and hardly any prep for a quick nostalgic bowl of the soup I grew up on.

COOKING TIME: 11 MINUTES — SERVES 6

2 tbsp (30 ml) extra virgin olive oil (EVOO), divided

1 lb (454 g) frozen ground beef

1 cup (240 ml) water

1 cup (160 g) diced onion

3 cloves garlic, diced

½ cup (64 g) diced carrot

½ cup (51 g) diced celery

½ cup (75 g) cubed potatoes or yuca

1 tbsp (15 ml) Paleo Worcestershire sauce

2 large dried whole bay leaves

1 tbsp (7 g) Italian seasoning

½ tsp sea salt

½ tsp freshly ground black pepper

1 (28-oz [790-g]) can diced tomatoes and juice

2 cups (480 ml) beef stock

2 tbsp (8 g) chopped fresh parsley

Turn on the Instant Pot by pressing "Sauté" and set to "More." Insert the inner pot and wait until the panel says "Hot."

Add 1 tablespoon (15 ml) of EVOO to the inner pot, and when the oil is hot, carefully add the frozen ground beef to brown for about 1 minute on each side. Add the water to the inner pot.

Press "Cancel." Close the lid tightly and move the steam release handle to "Sealing." Press the "Pressure Cooker/Manual" button and set the timer for 5 minutes on HIGH pressure.

When the timer ends, carefully turn the steam release handle to "Venting," press "Cancel" and allow the Instant Pot to depressurize until the float valve drops down. Open the lid carefully.

Transfer the meat to a cutting board, and drain the water from the inner pot. Chop the meat into smaller pieces with a knife. The meat won't be totally defrosted at this point, but you should be able to cut through with a sharp knife. Wipe down the inner pot and put it back in the Instant Pot. Press "Sauté" and set to "More."

Add the remaining EVOO to the inner pot, and sauté the onion, garlic, carrot, celery and potatoes for 2 minutes. Add the beef back to the inner pot and stir. Add the Worcestershire sauce, bay leaves, Italian seasoning, sea salt, black pepper, tomatoes and stock. Stir to combine. Press "Cancel." Close the lid tightly and move the steam release handle to "Sealing." Press the "Pressure Cooker/Manual" button and set the timer for 3 minutes on HIGH pressure.

When the timer ends, press "Cancel" and allow the Instant Pot to cool down naturally until the float valve drops down. Open the lid carefully and remove the bay leaves. Stir the soup to mix and ladle it into 6 bowls. Garnish with parsley before serving.

Dairy-Free Zuppa Toscana

This popular Tuscan soup can feed a small town because it is rich, hearty and creamy. I substituted dairy cream with coconut cream and you can't even tell the difference. If you can't tolerate potatoes, you can substitute it with yuca or parsnips and it's still very rich and comforting. Make a huge batch, grab a big ladle and tell everyone on the block, "Soup's on!"

COOKING TIME: 16 MINUTES — SERVES 8

5 strips of fresh or frozen bacon

1 lb (454 g) frozen Italian sausages

1 tbsp (15 ml) extra virgin olive oil (EVOO)

½ cup (80 g) diced onion

5 cloves garlic, crushed

3 cups (720 ml) unsalted chicken broth or stock

1 cup (100 g) frozen or fresh cauliflower florets

½ lb (226 g) potatoes, yuca or parsnips, cut into 1-inch (2.5-cm) cubes

1 tsp sea salt

1 tsp freshly ground black pepper

1 tsp Italian seasoning

¼ cup (15 g) chopped fresh parsley, divided

½ lb (226 g) chopped fresh kale leaves, stems discarded

1 cup (240 ml) full-fat coconut cream

¼ cup (20 g) grated Pecorino Romano cheese, plus more to taste (optional)

Turn on the Instant Pot by pressing "Sauté" and set to "More." Insert the inner pot and wait until the panel says "Hot."

Add the bacon to the inner pot, and sauté until the fat begins to render. Carefully add the frozen Italian sausages to brown for about 1 minute on each side. Using a slotted spoon or tongs, take out the bacon and the sausages and drain excess grease from the pot. Transfer the sausages onto a cutting board and chop them into smaller pieces with a knife. The meat won't be totally defrosted at this point, but you should be able to cut through with a sharp knife.

Put the inner pot back in the Instant Pot and press "Sauté" and set to "More." Add the EVOO, onion and garlic. Sauté for 2 minutes or until the onion is soft. Then, add the bacon, sausages, broth, cauliflower, potatoes, sea salt, black pepper, Italian seasoning and 2 tablespoons (8 g) of parsley. Close the lid tightly and move the steam release handle to "Sealing."

Press the "Pressure Cooker/Manual" button and set the timer for 10 minutes on HIGH pressure.

When the timer ends, press "Cancel" and allow the Instant Pot to cool down naturally until the float valve drops down. Open the lid carefully.

Press "Sauté." Add the kale, coconut cream, and Pecorino Romano cheese (if using). Stir for 2 minutes or until the kale wilts.

When ready to serve, press "Cancel," ladle the soup into bowls and garnish with the remaining parsley. Add extra Pecorino Romano cheese on top, if using.

Italian Sausage and Escarole Soup

There is a local Italian restaurant where we used to order escarole soup regularly before the ownership changed. Luckily, before the original owner left I got his recipe and I was grateful because it became my favorite Italian soup. The original version includes cannellini beans, but I Paleotized it with cauliflower florets and I think it tastes even better!

COOKING TIME: 6 MINUTES — SERVES 4

2 tbsp (30 ml) extra virgin olive oil (EVOO), divided

1 lb (454 g) frozen Italian sweet sausages

½ cup (80 g) diced onion

5 cloves garlic, crushed

1 lb (454 g) escarole, roughly chopped

1 cup (100 g) frozen cauliflower florets

3 cups (720 ml) chicken stock

¼ cup (15 g) chopped fresh parsley, divided

¼ cup (6 g) chopped fresh basil

1 tsp dried Italian seasoning

1 tsp sea salt

1 tsp freshly ground black pepper

1 tsp crushed red pepper (optional)

¼ cup (20 g) grated Pecorino Romano cheese (optional)

Turn on the Instant Pot by pressing "Sauté" and set to "More." Insert the inner pot and wait until the panel says "Hot."

Add 1 tablespoon (15 ml) of EVOO to the inner pot, and when the oil is hot, carefully add the frozen Italian sweet sausages to brown for about 1 minute. Using tongs, lift the sausages out of the inner pot and transfer to a cutting board. The sausages won't be totally defrosted at this point, but you should be able to cut them into 1- to 1½-inch (2- to 2.5-cm) pieces with a sharp knife.

Add the remaining EVOO to the inner pot. When the oil is hot, add the sausages, onion and garlic. Sauté for 1 minute or until the onion is soft. Add the escarole and cauliflower and sauté for 1 minute. Add the stock, parsley (reserve 1 tablespoon [4 g] for garnish), basil, Italian seasoning, sea salt, black pepper and crushed red pepper (if using).

Press "Cancel." Close the lid tightly and move the steam release handle to "Sealing." Press the "Pressure Cooker/Manual" button and set the timer for 3 minutes on HIGH pressure.

When the timer ends, press "Cancel" and allow the Instant Pot to cool down naturally until the float valve drops down. Open the lid carefully.

Stir the soup to mix and ladle it into 4 bowls. Garnish with the remaining parsley and Pecorino Romano cheese (if using) before serving.

Detoxifying Short Ribs and Radish Soup

I used to make a huge pot of this soup on the stove top, but it always took hours. Not anymore! I make this soup in the Instant Pot now at a fraction of the time and we eat it for days. It's so refreshing and nourishing. Even with frozen short ribs, it always makes tender, fall-off-the-bone and nourishing beef soup. I think it's even more flavorful than when it's made on the stove top! If you love bone broth, you'll love this meaty soup with detoxifying radish.

COOKING TIME: 45 MINUTES — SERVES 6

2 lbs (907 g) frozen short ribs

1 large onion, sliced thick

6 cloves garlic, crushed

1 tbsp (18 g) sea salt

1 tsp freshly ground black pepper

4 cups (960 ml) cold water

2 lbs (907 g) Korean radish or Daikon, cut into 1-inch (2.5-cm) cubes

5 scallions (4 sliced diagonally in 2-inch [5-cm] pieces, 1 chopped in ½-inch [1-cm] pieces)

Place the short ribs in the inner pot of the Instant Pot and fill with enough water to submerge the bones. Soak the bones in the water for 30 minutes at room temperature. Drain the water, add fresh water and repeat until the water runs clear. If the bones are not separated, this is a good time to separate each bone from the other bones.

Add the short ribs, onion, garlic, sea salt, black pepper and cold water to the inner pot. Close the lid tightly and move the steam release handle to "Sealing." Press the "Pressure Cooker/Manual" button and set the timer for 40 minutes on HIGH pressure.

When the timer ends, allow the Instant Pot to cool down naturally for 10 minutes. Open the lid carefully and add the radish and the long scallion pieces. Press the "Pressure Cooker/Manual" button and set the timer to 5 minutes.

When the timer ends, allow the Instant Pot to cool down naturally until the float valve drops down. Because there is a large amount of liquid and fat, this could take up to 30 minutes or longer, but you can open the lid after 30 minutes. Press "Cancel" and carefully open the lid.

Ladle the soup into bowls and garnish with the reserved chopped scallion. Serve immediately.

NOTE: *If you don't want to wait to add the radish pieces later, you can cut them bigger and add them in the beginning with the short ribs. The radish pieces will be much softer, but this will eliminate the extra step of adding them later.*

Savory Calamari Stew

Squid was once an ignored seafood that no one wanted. It wasn't a very popular menu item at restaurants and was definitely not a frequently requested dish at home. That has changed a lot in recent years—and so did the prices. The cat is out of the bag, so to speak, that squid is low in calories and fat, but it is high in protein. It is also rich in selenium, zinc and vitamin B$_{12}$ so it's so healthy for you. Fresh squid is great to cook because it cooks so quickly. If you feel squeamish about handling this slimy cephalopod, buy them frozen for a quick soup like this. I bet your family will request it from now on.

COOKING TIME: 4 MINUTES — SERVES 4

¼ cup (60 ml) extra virgin olive oil (EVOO), divided

1 cup (160 g) sliced onion

3 cloves garlic, crushed

10 oz (283 g) fennel bulb, sliced

1 fresh jalapeño pepper, chopped

2 lbs (907 g) frozen baby squid, cut in rings and tentacles

2 cups (228 g) frozen cauliflower rice

6 oz (170 g) tomato paste

1 cup (180 g) crushed tomatoes

1 tsp sea salt

½ tsp freshly ground black pepper

1 large dried whole bay leaf

1 tsp Italian seasoning

¼ cup (15 g) chopped fresh parsley, divided

1 tbsp (15 ml) fish sauce

½ cup (120 ml) good-quality dry red wine

¼ cup (20 g) Pecorino Romano cheese (optional)

Turn on the Instant Pot by pressing "Sauté" and set to "More." Insert the inner pot and wait until the panel says "Hot."

Add 2 tablespoons (30 ml) of EVOO to the inner pot. When the oil is hot, add the onion, garlic, fennel and jalapeño pepper. Sauté for 1 minute or until the onion is soft. Add the squid, cauliflower rice, tomato paste, crushed tomatoes, sea salt, black pepper, bay leaf, Italian seasoning, parsley (reserve 1 tablespoon [4 g] for garnish), fish sauce and red wine to the inner pot.

Press "Cancel." Close the lid tightly and move the steam release handle to "Sealing." Press the "Pressure Cooker/Manual" button and set the timer for 3 minutes on LOW pressure.

When the timer ends, carefully turn the steam release handle to "Venting," press "Cancel" and allow the Instant Pot to depressurize quickly until the float valve drops down. Open the lid carefully.

Remove the bay leaf. Add the Pecorino Romano cheese (if using) to the soup and stir. Ladle the soup into bowls and garnish with the remaining parsley. Drizzle with the remaining EVOO and serve immediately.

Vegetable Mulligatawny Soup

Mulligatawny soup translates to "pepper water." It is a soup which originated from southern India and was popular in England during the British occupation of India. While the British started adding meat to the soup, the original version did not include meat. In fact, bestselling Indian cookbook author, Archana Mundhe loves the Chicken Mulligatawny Soup from my second cookbook, Keto Cooking with Your Instant Pot®, *and she said her family asks for it often. This time, to keep in line with the original version that doesn't include meat, I've created this recipe using frozen vegetables. You can add more pepper for an even more authentic taste!*

COOKING TIME: 4 MINUTES — SERVES 8

¼ cup (52 g) ghee

½ cup (80 g) diced onion

1 (1-inch [2.5-cm]) piece of fresh ginger, minced

½ tsp crushed red pepper

1 fresh jalapeño or chili pepper, sliced

1 tsp sea salt

1 tsp freshly ground black pepper

⅛ tsp ground nutmeg

¼ tsp dried thyme

2 tsp (4 g) curry powder

½ cup (51 g) chopped celery

1 cup (128 g) frozen sliced carrots (or fresh)

2 cups (200 g) frozen cauliflower florets

1 cup (150 g) cubed frozen white potatoes or sweet potatoes

2 cups (480 ml) vegetable stock

¼ cup (4 g) chopped fresh cilantro, divided

2 cups (480 ml) full-fat coconut milk

Turn on the Instant Pot by pressing "Sauté" and set to "More." Insert the inner pot and wait until the panel says "HOT." Melt the ghee in the inner pot and add the onion, ginger, crushed red pepper and jalapeño pepper. Sauté for 1 minute or until the onion is soft. Add the sea salt, black pepper, nutmeg, thyme, curry powder, celery, carrots, cauliflower, potatoes, stock and cilantro (reserve 1 tablespoon [1 g] for garnish). Hit "Cancel."

Close the lid tightly and move the steam release handle to "Sealing." Press the "Pressure Cooker/Manual" button and set the timer for 3 minutes on HIGH pressure.

When the timer ends, press "Cancel" and allow the Instant Pot to cool down naturally until the float valve drops down. Open the lid carefully.

Stir in the coconut milk and reserved cilantro. Ladle the soup into bowls, garnish with the remaining cilantro and serve immediately.

Cioppino for a Crowd

I always think of exotic seaside towns in Italy when I make this soup. The name is derived from soups made in various towns in Italy, but this is actually an American soup! Regardless, the combination of a variety of seafood used in this quintessential soup was meant to be served with sourdough bread. You can use any Paleo bread to sop up the last bit of broth.

COOKING TIME: 10 MINUTES — SERVES 8

½ cup (80 g) diced onion

3 cloves garlic, crushed

8 anchovy fillets in oil

1 cup (128 g) sliced carrots (1-inch [2.5-cm] pieces)

1 cup (101 g) sliced celery (1-inch [2.5-cm] pieces)

1 cup (180 g) diced tomatoes

2 tbsp (32 g) tomato paste

1 tbsp (15 ml) fish sauce

½ cup (120 ml) good-quality dry white wine

1 cup (240 ml) fish stock

1 tsp Italian seasoning

2 large dried whole bay leaves

¼ cup (15 g) chopped fresh parsley, divided

6 frozen or fresh little neck clams, de-sanded and washed

1 lb (454 g) frozen or fresh mussels, de-sanded and washed

½ lb (226 g) frozen large shrimp with shells

½ lb (226 g) frozen squid rings and tentacles

6 large frozen scallops

½ lb (226 g) frozen or fresh cod or other meaty fish, cut into 2-inch (5-cm) chunks

1 tbsp (15 ml) extra virgin olive oil (EVOO)

Insert the inner pot and add the onion, garlic, anchovy fillets, carrots, celery, tomatoes, tomato paste, fish sauce, wine, stock, Italian seasoning, bay leaves and parsley (reserve 1 tablespoon [4 g] for garnish). Stir. Then, in this order, add and spread the clams, mussels, shrimp, squid and scallops, then add the cod fillets last.

Close the lid tightly and move the steam release handle to "Sealing." Turn on the Instant Pot by pressing the "Pressure Cooker/Manual" button. Set the timer for 10 minutes on LOW pressure.

When the timer ends, carefully turn the steam release handle to "Venting," press "Cancel," and allow the Instant Pot to depressurize quickly until the float valve drops down. Open the lid carefully.

Ladle the soup into bowls, with a variety of seafood added to each bowl. Garnish with the remaining parsley, drizzle with EVOO, and serve immediately.

Rotisserie Chicken Soup

I have no shame in admitting that I occasionally buy cooked rotisserie chicken in a pinch. If you are like me, you do the same and you have a bag of at least two carcasses sitting in the freezer. Am I right? Well then, this is the perfect chicken soup for you and you will be proud to admit you make the best and fastest chicken soup on the block. Don't worry. Your secret is safe with me.

COOKING TIME: 15 MINUTES — SERVES 6

1 medium onion, sliced thick

2 ribs celery, sliced into 1-inch (2.5-cm) pieces

2 carrots, sliced into 1-inch (2.5-cm) pieces

2 cups (300 g) russet potato, yuca, turnips or radish, cut into 2-inch (5-cm) cubes (optional)

2 large dried whole bay leaves

¼ cup (15 g) chopped fresh parsley, divided

1 tsp dried oregano

1 tsp dried thyme

1 tsp dried rosemary

1 tsp dried tarragon

3 cloves garlic, crushed

1 tbsp (18 g) sea salt

1 tsp freshly ground black pepper

3 cups (720 ml) water

2 frozen rotisserie chicken carcasses, broken up

To the inner pot, add the onion, celery, carrots, potatoes (if using), bay leaves, parsley (reserve 2 tablespoons [8 g] for garnish), oregano, thyme, rosemary, tarragon, garlic, sea salt, black pepper, water and carcasses. The carcasses should be nestled in the vegetables and submerged in water.

Close the lid tightly and move the steam release handle to "Sealing." Turn on the Instant Pot by pressing the "Pressure Cooker/Manual" button and set the timer for 15 minutes on HIGH pressure.

When the timer ends, press "Cancel" and allow the Instant Pot to cool down naturally until the float valve drops down. Open the lid carefully.

Remove the bay leaves and crush the carrots and celery gently against the side of the pot with the back of a spoon. Add more sea salt and black pepper, if needed. Ladle the soup into bowls and garnish with the remaining parsley before serving.

Vietnamese Chicken Noodle Soup (Pho)

You can't talk about noodle soup without mentioning this classic Vietnamese dish, Pho (pronounced "fuh"). Its aromatic taste comes from dry roasting some of the herbs and spices before adding the other ingredients to make the broth. If you can tolerate rice noodles, this recipe is the perfect noodle soup for you.

COOKING TIME: 23 MINUTES — SERVES 6

2 frozen skinless, boneless chicken breasts (½ lb [226 g])

1 tsp of ground cinnamon

½ tsp of ground coriander

½ tsp coriander seeds

½ tsp whole cloves

1 whole star anise, crushed

1 medium onion, roughly chopped

1 (3-inch [7.5-cm]) piece of fresh ginger, peeled and chopped

1 tsp crushed red pepper flakes

4 cloves garlic, roughly chopped

1 cup (16 g) roughly chopped fresh cilantro, roots, stems and leaves, divided

1 tbsp (15 ml) tamari or coconut aminos

1 tbsp (15 ml) fish sauce

5 cups (1.2 L) chicken stock

4 servings of dried rice noodles or zoodles (See the Noodles Tip on page 126)

4 scallions, thinly sliced

1 cup (100 g) raw bean sprouts (optional)

2 fresh jalapeño peppers, sliced

6 lime wedges

Take the frozen chicken breasts out of the freezer and rinse them with cold running water to separate them. Set them aside on a sheet pan.

Turn on the Instant Pot by pressing "Sauté" and set to "More." Insert the inner pot and wait until the panel says "Hot." In the inner pot, add the cinnamon, ground coriander, coriander seeds, cloves and star anise. Sauté for about 5 minutes or until fragrant and smoky. Stir constantly so as not to burn them. Add the onion, ginger and crushed red pepper. Sauté for 2 minutes. Add the garlic, cilantro (reserve 6 teaspoons [2 g] for garnish), tamari, fish sauce and the stock. Stir.

Put the chicken breasts in, close the lid tightly and move the steam release handle to "Sealing." Press "Cancel," then press the "Pressure Cooker/ Manual" button and set the timer for 15 minutes on HIGH pressure.

Meanwhile, put the rice noodles in a large bowl with cold water.

When the timer ends, carefully turn the steam release handle to "Venting," press "Cancel" and allow the Instant Pot to depressurize quickly until the float valve drops down. Open the lid carefully.

Take out the chicken breasts and shred them on a cutting board. Place the rice noodles in bowls. Strain the pho broth into the bowls. Top the bowls with shredded chicken, scallions, 1 teaspoon of the reserved cilantro, bean sprouts (if using), jalapeño peppers and a lime wedge before serving.

NOTE: *Coconut aminos can vary in sodium content, depending on whether the bottle is labeled as "sauce" or just plain coconut aminos. This recipe uses plain coconut aminos with 130 mg sodium per 5 ml.*

"Cream" of Broccoli Soup

When Socrates said, "let food be thy medicine and medicine be thy food," I'm sure he was referring to this soup. This is like slurping vitamins and antioxidants because broccoli is rich in both. Leek adds mellow sweetness to the broccoli, and cashew cream adds a velvety texture. This soup will change any broccoli haters into broccoli lovers while nourishing them without them even knowing it.

COOKING TIME: 7 MINUTES — SERVES 4

1 cup raw cashew nuts (See Note for substitution)

2 tbsp (26 g) ghee

1 cup (90 g) sliced leek whites and tender greens

½ cup (80 g) diced onion

2 large cloves garlic, crushed

2 cups (312 g) frozen broccoli florets and sliced stems

2 cups (480 ml) unsalted chicken broth

1 sprig of fresh tarragon, leaves removed and stems discarded or 2 tsp (2 g) dried tarragon

Sea salt and freshly ground pepper, to taste

¼ cup (60 ml) full-fat coconut cream

2 tsp (2 g) chopped fresh chives

Soak the raw cashews in cold water for 30 minutes. After they're soaked, drain the water and set aside. Discard the water.

Turn on the Instant Pot by pressing "Sauté" and set to "More." Insert the inner pot and wait until the panel says "Hot." Melt the ghee and sauté the leeks, onion and garlic for 3 minutes or until the leeks are soft. Add the cashews, broccoli, broth and tarragon to the inner pot.

Close the lid tightly and move the steam release handle to "Sealing." Press "Cancel," then press the "Pressure Cooker/Manual" button and set the timer for 4 minutes on HIGH pressure.

When the timer ends, turn the steam release handle to the "Venting" position for the steam to escape and the float valve to drop down. Press "Cancel" and carefully open the lid.

Using an immersion blender or a regular blender, purée the soup until smooth. Add sea salt and pepper, to taste, drizzle with coconut cream and garnish with chives before serving.

NOTE: *If you have a nut allergy, you can substitute cashews for 1 cup (114 g) of cauliflower rice or florets and add 1 tablespoon (8 g) of tapioca flour to the soup to thicken.*

Bacon Cheeseburger and Mushrooms Soup

If you can't grill burgers outside and don't want the mess around the stove, you'll love this soup. It has all the elements of a hefty bacon cheeseburger with mushrooms, and it makes a great meal without the mess!

COOKING TIME: 7 MINUTES — SERVES 6

3 strips of bacon, chopped

1 lb (454 g) frozen ground beef

1 tbsp (13 g) ghee

1 medium onion, diced

3 cloves garlic, crushed

1 cup (70 g) sliced white mushrooms

1 cup (70 g) thinly sliced green cabbage

1 tbsp Paleo Worcestershire sauce

1 large dried whole bay leaf

1 tsp Italian seasoning

¼ cup (15 g) chopped fresh parsley, divided

½ cup (90 g) crushed tomatoes

2 tbsp (32 g) tomato paste

½ cup (120 ml) good-quality dry red wine

1 cup (240 ml) unsalted beef stock

1 tsp sea salt

1 tsp freshly ground black pepper

¼ cup (32 g) nutritional yeast or Pecorino Romano cheese

Turn on the Instant Pot by pressing "Sauté" and set to "More." Insert the inner pot and wait until the panel says "Hot."

Add the bacon to the inner pot and sauté until it begins to render fat and get crispy. Take out a few bacon pieces and set aside to use as garnish. Carefully add the frozen ground beef and cook for about 1 minute on each side until the sides are opaque. Using tongs, transfer the ground beef to a cutting board and chop the meat into smaller pieces with a knife. The meat won't be totally defrosted at this point, but you should be able to cut through it with a sharp knife.

Add the ghee to the inner pot. Add the onion and garlic, and sauté for 1 minute. Add the beef back to the inner pot and stir. Add the mushrooms, cabbage, Worcestershire sauce, bay leaf, Italian seasoning, 2 tablespoons (8 g) of parsley, tomatoes, tomato paste, red wine, stock, sea salt and black pepper.

Press "Cancel." Close the lid tightly and move the steam release handle to "Sealing." Press the "Pressure Cooker/Manual" button and set the timer for 5 minutes on HIGH pressure.

When the timer ends, press "Cancel" and allow the Instant Pot to cool down naturally until the float valve drops down. Open the lid carefully.

Remove the bay leaf. Stir the soup to mix and ladle it into bowls. Garnish with the remaining parsley, bacon pieces and nutritional yeast before serving.

Chicken and Dumplings Soup

The funny story about chicken and dumplings soup is that we always had real dumplings and not lumps of cooked dough in the chicken soup. So, whenever I saw this recipe title, I didn't want to make it because I was too lazy to make the dumplings. One day, my daughter had leftover dough in the fridge after making hand pulled noodles. So, she decided to add them to a chicken soup to use it up and discovered she inadvertently made chicken and dumplings soup! And now, it's one of our favorite soups! See how wonderful things get discovered by accident?

COOKING TIME: 15 MINUTES — SERVES 6

SOUP

2 lbs (907 g) frozen boneless, skinless chicken thighs

2 carrots, cut into 1-inch (2.5-cm) pieces

2 ribs celery, cut into 1-inch (2.5-cm) pieces

1 lb (454 g) white potatoes or yuca, cut in 2-inch (5-cm) cubes

¼ cup (15 g) chopped fresh parsley, divided

1 tsp dried tarragon

1 tsp dried thyme

1 tsp dried oregano

3 cups (720 ml) unsalted chicken broth

1 tsp sea salt

½ tsp freshly ground black pepper

1 tbsp (8 g) tapioca flour

¼ cup (60 ml) cold water

DUMPLINGS

½ cup (70 g) cassava flour

½ cup (52 g) ultra-fine blanched almond flour

½ tsp baking soda

1 tbsp (8 g) tapioca flour

½ tsp sea salt

½ cup (120 ml) cold water

Add the chicken thighs, carrots, celery, potatoes, parsley (reserve 1 tablespoon [4 g] for garnish), tarragon, thyme, oregano, broth, sea salt and black pepper to the inner pot. Close the lid tightly and move the steam release handle to "Sealing." Turn on the Instant Pot by pressing the "Pressure Cooker/Manual" button and set the timer for 10 minutes on HIGH pressure.

Meanwhile, make a slurry by combining the tapioca flour and cold water. Set aside.

In a medium-sized mixing bowl, combine the cassava flour, almond flour, baking soda, tapioca flour, sea salt and water to make a dough. Take about 1 tablespoon (15 g) of the dough at a time and flatten it to make round disks and set aside.

When the timer ends, press "Cancel" and allow the Instant Pot to cool down naturally until the float valve drops down. Open the lid carefully.

Transfer the chicken to a cutting board and cut into small bite-size pieces. Add the slurry to the inner pot and stir until the soup thickens. Press "Sauté" and drop the "dumplings" in one at a time and stir. Add the chicken pieces back to the inner pot and simmer for 5 minutes while stirring occasionally. Press "Cancel."

Ladle the soup into bowls, garnish with the remaining parsley and serve immediately.

> NOTE: *This Paleo chicken and dumplings soup is not as thick as the traditional version. The chicken is not floured or browned, and it only has tapioca slurry and dumplings at the end. If you don't want to bother with adding the tapioca slurry, you can omit that. Just add the dumplings at the end before serving.*

Mrs. Chen's Egg Drop Soup

I don't know about you, but I used to add beaten egg to chicken broth and called it egg drop soup. But after I learned how to make it right from my neighbor, Mrs. Chen who owns a Chinese restaurant, I don't take shortcuts anymore. Personally, I think this version tastes better than any restaurant's egg drop soup, even Mrs. Chen's, because it has no sugar or corn syrup. But shhh . . . don't tell her that.

COOKING TIME: 15 MINUTES — SERVES 4

4 frozen chicken thighs

3 whole scallions, divided

1 (1-inch [2.5-cm]) piece of fresh ginger, sliced

1 tsp sea salt

1 tbsp (8 g) tapioca flour

2 cups (480 ml) chicken stock

3 large eggs, slightly beaten

1 tsp white pepper

½ tsp ground turmeric

1 tsp sesame oil

¼ cup (4 g) chopped fresh cilantro stems and leaves, divided

Add the chicken thighs, 2 scallions, ginger, sea salt and 2¾ cups (660 ml) of water to the inner pot. Close the lid tightly and move the steam release handle to "Sealing." Turn on the Instant Pot by pressing the "Pressure Cooker/Manual" button and set the timer for 10 minutes on HIGH pressure.

Meanwhile, make a slurry by combining the tapioca flour and ¼ cup (60 ml) cold water. Set aside. Finely chop the reserved scallion for garnish.

When the timer ends, press "Cancel" and allow the Instant Pot to cool down naturally until the float valve drops down. Open the lid carefully.

Transfer the chicken to a cutting board, debone and cut the meat into small bite-size pieces. Strain the broth and discard the chicken bones, the ginger and long scallions. Add the broth back to the inner pot, then add the 2 cups (480 ml) of chicken stock. Press "Sauté." Add the slurry and chicken pieces back to the inner pot. Simmer for 5 minutes while stirring occasionally. Slowly drizzle the beaten eggs into the soup while stirring gently. Add the white pepper, turmeric, sesame oil and cilantro (reserve 1 tablespoon [1 g] for garnish).

Press "Cancel," ladle the soup into bowls. Garnish with the remaining cilantro and chopped scallions, and serve immediately.

Leaves and Roots

I wish we could always have fresh vegetables, but unless you live in a warm climate, you have to resort to vegetables flown in from far away or rely on frozen vegetables. I eat vegetables seasonally, but I freeze some of them to save their freshness all year round. Not all frozen vegetables cook well because they end up being too soft, but root vegetables, such as beets, parsnips, carrots, Brussels sprouts and even cauli rice, can be cooked to perfection.

You'll love the Roasted Cauliflower and Beet Hummus (page 181). It's even better than chickpea hummus. The Beets and Pink Grapefruit Salad with Citrus Dressing (page 174) is so easy to make in the Instant Pot using frozen beets. And of course, there's everyone's favorite Cauliflower and Parsnip Purée (page 178)—but for a bit of nuttiness I added parsnips. These dishes make great sides, but I've been known to have a small bowl as a meal on a busy night.

Beets and Pink Grapefruit Salad with Citrus Dressing

I am lucky to live in an area where I can buy beets any time of the year. But, there's nothing like fresh beets in the summer. Still, no matter how much I love beets, I can't finish all of them. So I freeze some to use throughout the year. Frozen beets cook beautifully in the pressure cooker, and they are perfect with citrus fruits in the winter when citrus is in season. Try this gorgeous salad any time of the year. It's so easy and delicious!

COOKING TIME: 15 MINUTES — SERVES 4

4 small whole frozen beets

4 large orange zest strips, about 2 inches (5 cm) each

1 tbsp (9 g) orange zest

½ cup (120 ml) orange juice

½ cup (120 ml) grapefruit juice or juice from one grapefruit

3 tbsp (45 ml) apple cider vinegar, divided

1 large pink grapefruit

2 tsp (10 ml) Dijon mustard

1 tbsp (15 ml) raw honey

6 fresh mint leaves, half of the leaves finely chopped

1 tsp lemon zest

Take the frozen beets out of the freezer, run them through cold water and clean them gently. Put the washed beets in the inner pot of the Instant Pot. Add the orange zest strips, orange zest, orange juice, grapefruit juice and 2 tablespoons (30 ml) of vinegar to the inner pot.

Close the lid tightly and move the steam release handle to "Sealing." Press the "Pressure Cooker/ Manual" button and set the timer for 15 minutes on HIGH pressure.

Meanwhile, using a sharp paring knife, peel the grapefruit and cut away all the white pith underneath. Then, hold the peeled grapefruit in your non-dominant hand, and cut each segment as close to each white membrane with your dominant hand, carefully removing the segments onto a serving platter. When you have all of the segments, cover and refrigerate.

When the timer ends, carefully turn the steam release handle to the "Venting" position for the steam to escape and the float valve to drop down. Press "Cancel" and carefully open the lid.

Remove and discard the zest strips. Remove the beets from the inner pot and transfer to a cutting board. Slice the beets in ½-inch (1-cm) thick slices, place the slices in between the grapefruit segments on a platter and refrigerate. You can prepare the beets and grapefruit, up until this point, days ahead and plate them just before serving.

Add the remaining vinegar, Dijon mustard, honey and chopped mint leaves to the inner pot with the citrus liquid, and stir until they are incorporated.

Take out the platter of beets and grapefruit, and drizzle with the citrus dressing from the inner pot. Sprinkle with lemon zest and garnish with unchopped mint before serving.

Vegetarian Shepherd's Pie

Using pre-cut frozen vegetables changed my cooking forever. This recipe takes so little time to make in the Instant Pot. In fact, gathering the herbs and spices out of the cupboard might take you longer than prepping the veggies! It's such a quick meal on a busy night, and you might have to fight your family to have enough for lunch the next day. It's truly a win-win dish!

COOKING TIME: 3 MINUTES — SERVES 6

2 cups (about 400 g) Cauliflower and Parsnip Purée (page 178)

2 tbsp (26 g) ghee, divided

½ cup (80 g) diced onion

3 cloves garlic, crushed

2 cups (140 g) sliced white mushrooms

½ cup (120 ml) good-quality dry red wine

1 cup (240 ml) unsalted vegetable stock

½ cup (64 g) frozen diced carrots

1 cup (129 g) frozen pearl onions

½ cup (55 g) frozen green beans, sliced into ½-inch (1-cm) pieces

1 cup (100 g) frozen cauliflower florets

½ cup (51 g) diced celery

2 cups (140 g) sliced green or purple cabbage

1 large dried whole bay leaf

1 tsp dried thyme

1 tsp dried tarragon

¼ cup (15 g) chopped fresh parsley, divided

1 tsp sea salt

¼ tsp freshly ground black pepper

1 tbsp (8 g) tapioca flour, plus more if needed

¼ cup (60 ml) cold water, plus more if needed

Make the purée and set it aside.

Turn on the Instant Pot by pressing "Sauté" and set to "More." Insert the inner pot and wait until the panel says "Hot."

Add 1 tablespoon (13 g) of ghee to the inner pot and when it's hot, add the onion and garlic. Sauté for 1 minute, then add the mushrooms and stir. Pour the red wine and deglaze the bottom of the pot. Add the stock, carrots, pearl onions, green beans, cauliflower, celery, cabbage, bay leaf, thyme, tarragon, parsley (reserve 1 tablespoon [4 g] for garnish), sea salt and black pepper.

Press "Cancel." Close the lid tightly and move the steam release handle to "Sealing." Press the "Pressure Cooker/Manual" button and set the timer for 1 minute on HIGH pressure.

Meanwhile, combine the tapioca flour and water in a small bowl to make a slurry. Set aside.

When the timer ends, carefully turn the steam release handle to "Venting," press "Cancel" and allow the Instant Pot to depressurize quickly until the float valve drops down. Open the lid carefully.

Remove the bay leaf. Stir the tapioca slurry into the pot and stir to thicken. Make more slurry, if needed, to achieve your desired thickness. Allow the vegetables to simmer for 2 to 3 minutes.

Turn the oven on to the "Broil" setting. Transfer the vegetable mixture to a 9 x 9–inch (23 x 23–cm) glass ovenproof pan and spread the prepared purée evenly on top. Brush the top with the remaining ghee. Place the pan under the broiler for 2 to 3 minutes or until the purée turns golden brown. Garnish with the remaining parsley before serving.

Cauliflower and Parsnip Purée

I could literally eat this dish all by myself as a meal. It's creamy, silky, sweet and a bit nutty because of the parsnips. You can make this with frozen cauliflower and parsnips, so you don't even have to wash and cut veggies! If you grow vegetables in your garden, you can freeze parsnips for year-round eating. Also, you can easily find cauliflower as florets or riced in the frozen food section of your grocery store. Make this purée as a side dish or to top the Vegetarian Shepherd's Pie (page 177).

COOKING TIME: 4 MINUTES — SERVES 4

1 cup (240 ml) water

2 frozen whole parsnips

2 cups (200 g) frozen cauliflower florets or riced

½ tsp sea salt

2 tbsp (26 g) ghee

¼ cup (60 ml) full-fat coconut milk, plus more if needed

1 tbsp (4 g) chopped fresh parsley

Place the water and a wired vegetable steamer (or a glass or stainless-steel bowl on a trivet) in the inner pot. Place the parsnips and cauliflower in the steamer (or in the bowl on the trivet.) Close the lid tightly and move the steam release handle to "Sealing." Turn on the Instant Pot by pressing the "Pressure Cooker/Manual" button and set the timer for 4 minutes on HIGH pressure.

When the timer ends, carefully turn the steam release handle to "Venting," press "Cancel," and allow the Instant Pot to depressurize quickly until the float valve drops down. Open the lid carefully.

Transfer the vegetables to a blender or a food processor. Add sea salt, ghee and coconut milk. Blend. Add more coconut milk, if needed. Garnish with the parsley and serve immediately.

Roasted Cauliflower and Beet Hummus

Hummus is a great dip, but it's made with chickpeas—which are not Paleo-friendly. I prefer this silky cauliflower hummus over the conventional hummus any day. I added beets for the pretty color and to add some earthy flavors. No one would know this is not made with chickpeas! But then, they may like this even better!

COOKING TIME: 19 MINUTES — SERVES 4

1 lb (454 g) fresh cauliflower florets

2 tbsp (30 ml) extra virgin olive oil (EVOO)

1 tsp sea salt

½ tsp freshly ground black pepper

1 cup (240 ml) water

1 small (4 oz [113 g]) frozen beet

1 clove garlic, pressed or finely minced

¼ tsp ground cumin

2 tbsp (30 g) tahini

2 tbsp (6 g) finely chopped fresh chives, divided

¼ cup (60 ml) unsalted vegetable stock

Preheat the oven to 400°F (200°C, or gas mark 6). Place a rack in the middle of the oven.

Spread the cauliflower florets on an ovenproof sheet pan. Drizzle EVOO on the florets and coat evenly. Sprinkle sea salt and black pepper on the florets evenly. Place the sheet pan in the oven and roast the cauliflower for 10 to 15 minutes or until golden brown. Turn them over half way through the cooking time.

When the cauliflower florets are browned, take the sheet pan out and turn off the oven. Place the water and a wired vegetable steamer in the inner pot, or use a glass or stainless-steel bowl on a trivet. Place the beet and the roasted cauliflower in the steamer or in the bowl on the trivet.

Close the lid tightly and move the steam release handle to "Sealing." Meanwhile, turn on the Instant Pot by pressing the "Pressure Cooker/Manual" button and set the timer for 4 minutes on HIGH pressure. Insert the inner pot.

When the timer ends, carefully turn the steam release handle to "Venting," press "Cancel" and allow the Instant Pot to depressurize quickly until the float valve drops down. Open the lid carefully.

Using a slotted spoon, transfer the vegetables to a food processor or a blender. Add the garlic, cumin, tahini and 1 tablespoon (3 g) of chives. Pour in the stock little by little, watching for the right consistency. Add more stock, if needed. Transfer to a serving bowl, garnish with the remaining chives before serving.

NOTE: *You can store hummus in a tightly closed container and refrigerate for up to 2 weeks.*

Acknowledgments

Coming up with cookbook topics can take a long time. For this book, a friend I respect asked me to write a cookbook that tells her how she can "drop the frozen block of food in the Instant Pot and it just cooks it for me!" Well, after weeks of researching and experimenting, that didn't quite work out. Still, she gave me something to think about and I am so glad my publisher agreed that cooking with frozen ingredients would be a great topic for a cookbook. I think we all agree that more recipes that help make our busy lives easier are always welcome.

My husband: For constantly asking, "Are you done yet?" and keeping me focused on finishing the book. Cooking and eating are one thing, but writing is always challenging, and I really needed your "gentle" nudges when so many "life" interruptions got in the way while writing this book.

My children: Your famous question, "Is it cooked?" got me to recheck and rethink food safety issues for this cookbook. I raised some smart cookies, and I am proud to have you in my corner to make sure I write great cookbooks. You are my biggest cheerleaders and my biggest success.

My photographer/confidant Donna Crous: I couldn't have written another cookbook without your creative pair of eyes behind the lens. I am eternally grateful for your talent and for making my recipes come to life in print. I am so proud of our work together! Love you!

My lovely fellow Instant Pot cookbook authors and experts, Archana Mundhe, Barbara Schieving, Emily Sunwell-Vidaurri and Alyssa Brantley: your constant support and encouragement make me a better cook and recipe developer. I appreciate you ladies!

My Page Street editor and publisher, Marissa and William: Once again, you had the confidence in me to write another cookbook! Thank you for having faith in me! And thank you Meg and your creative team for the beautiful layout! You guys are the best in the publishing world!

Last but not least, to my friends, loyal readers and followers: Your constant support and cheerleading make me want to improve. Thank you for pre-orders, purchases and the wonderful feedback you leave everywhere. You don't know how much they elevate me on so many levels. Your demand for healthy recipes encourages me to develop delicious recipes and write better cookbooks. Thank you so much for your love! I appreciate you!

About Dr. Karen S. Lee

Dr. Karen S. Lee is a retired holistic practitioner with a Doctor of Chiropractic degree and is an Acupuncture and Oriental Medicine Fellow. Dr. Karen believes many illnesses can be reversed through being on a proper diet, supplements and stress management protocol. She's an author of many eBooks and the printed cookbooks, *Paleo Cooking with Your Air Fryer* and *Keto Cooking with Your Instant Pot®*.

You can find her work about holistic health, real food recipes and natural living tips on her website drkarenslee.com She lives with her family in Westchester, New York.

Follow @drkarenslee on: Facebook | Instagram | Pinterest | Twitter

Index